Life Outside the Box

Library and Archives Canada Cataloguing in Publication

Wilson, Marilyn R., 1955-, author
    Life outside the box : the extraordinary journeys of 10
unique individuals / Marilyn R. Wilson.

Issued in print and electronic formats.
ISBN 978-1-77141-066-3 (pbk.).--ISBN 978-1-77141-095-3 (html)

    1. Success--Case studies. 2. Successful people--Case studies.
I. Title.

BF637.S8W546 2014   650.1   C2014-906510-8
                                                  C2014-906511-6

Life Outside the Box

The Extraordinary Journeys of 10 Unique Individuals

Marilyn R. Wilson

Editing Team: Nina Shoroplova, Susan Kehoe
Typeset: Greg Salisbury
Book Cover Design: Adrian Horvath
Portrait Photographer: Eydís S. Luna Einardóttir / Studio 80s

Testimonials

"*Through the compelling stories of individuals who have made remarkable achievements by being true to themselves, this book shows how being yourself is the key to success.*"
Andy Chu, Executive Producer, FMA Entertainment

"*Wilson empathizes so passionately with her subjects that each exchange seems like a therapeutic chat with a lifelong friend. If only all writers could get through the bony chest plate and to the heart so effortlessly!*"
Darryl Humphrey, Professional Photographer

"*I admire Marilyn's commitment to finding and sharing an individual's life stories in a way we can all connect with and relate to. A wonderful book showcasing inspirational stories and journeys on the road less travelled.*"
**Tricia Romani, President,
Wilhelmina Models Vancouver**

"*Marilyn Wilson does everything with a full heart, this includes sharing the stories of 10 amazing individuals. Wilson's writing makes obvious her passion for her subjects. You'll feel the same at the end of Life Outside the Box.*"
Sarah Murray, Director, Fashion Capsule

"Marilyn Wilson is passionate about people – pure and simple. Combine that passion with her insatiable curiosity, genuine interest in the human journey and a gift for storytelling and you have someone you thoroughly enjoy – be it in-person or through her gifts with the written word. She inspires as surely as she derives inspiration from others."

Debra Walker, Author and Human Relations Specialist

"A book that will leave you feeling energized about life! Entertaining and thought provoking, the stories profiled are all about finding a purpose and creating a life of meaning and fulfillment."

Vladimir Markovich, Creative and Fashion Director

Acknowledgements

While there are many, many people who supported my journey, there are a few important thank-yous in particular I would like to mention here because of their direct involvement in this book.

To my wonderful husband of thirty years who has had to deal with all my stress as I stumble along to find this new direction—I know it hasn't been easy. Thanks for always having open arms when I need them.

To Julie, who came into my life at the perfect moment—earlier and I wouldn't have heard the call; later and I might have already walked away from writing. You still inspire me daily.

To Gulnar—your weekly check-ins and soft words of encouragement brought me out of the abyss of procrastination and kept me on track.

To Monika who not only gave me a push to succeed, but a solid knowledge of the potential of social media marketing and *The Secret*—you are my inspiration.

And lastly to Adrian Horvath, a truly talented graphic artist who honoured me by taking time out of his very busy schedule to create this amazing book cover—you have the patience of Job. From all the outside chaos of ideas that came your way, you quietly found that creative spark that knocked it out of the ballpark.

In closing, I also want to acknowledge the wonderful and insanely talented fashion community in Vancouver. I can't list all the names here as there are just way too many. You raised me up when I first entered your world, gave me focus and opportunity, held my hand through the self-doubt of writing this book, and then supported me in promoting it. I couldn't have done it without each and every one of you.

I am filled with gratitude. I am blessed.

Contents

Testimonials
Acknowledgements
Contents
Introduction

Introduction

A few months ago, I was floored to come across a photograph of myself in one of my old high school yearbooks. My memory is of the classic, consistently unhappy teenager who was not a joiner. I had a couple of friends to hang out with, but other than that I just couldn't wait to leave. In fact I graduated a year early and quickly headed off to university. But there I was, in a photo of that year's journalism club, smack dab in the middle of all these other students and glowing like I had a spotlight on me. Unbelievably, I was sporting an ear-to-ear smile. In fact, I was the one who looked the happiest. Was that really me? Viewing it, a sense of destiny washed over me.

Writing was meant to come into my life at just the right time. Pre-computer, it wouldn't have happened. The speed, easy corrections, and instant access to readers through the internet suited my temperament. In fact, my journey to writing started online. I was forty-nine and looking for a new interest, so decided to explore the job offers on Craigslist. One was from a New York fashion magazine looking for submissions. I knew a few local designers through my daughter's freelance modelling. Why not? I submitted three story ideas and two were accepted.

I had always had a deep-seated interest in the unique way people choose to live their lives, so it's no surprise that after my first interview with producer/designer Denise Brillon I was hooked. Listening to her share so openly about her life, there was a sense of time unfolding and in her words I found those first personal lessons to embrace. I had goose bumps by the end. When I walked outside, everything seemed just a bit brighter. What a privilege that she became not only a good friend, but a wonderful mentor. Writing a great magazine article would prove to be more challenging and to involve a definite learning curve. There were frequent tears of frustration, but it was worth it just to get the chance to hear these unique stories. Even today, it's the interviews I live for. Every single one of them changes me and how I look at my own life journey.

It became clear to me that, after over five years of my enjoying interviewing, writing, and co-owning a local magazine, the industry was in flux. Paycheques were few and far between, and ads hard to sell. Then my own magazine folded. The idea of self-publishing a book with mini-bios of some of my favourite interviews seemed a great direction as people enjoyed hearing all my interesting behind-the-scenes stories. The reality, however, was I needed deadlines and support to reach the finish line. That support came in the form of Julie Salisbury, Founder of Influence Publishing, a hybrid publisher.

It was intuition that led me to hear her speak at a women's networking night. I was tired and had almost decided to stay home when something deep inside drew me to get in the car. I will forever be grateful. I have heard others say when someone who was to become their mentor walked into the room, they felt a physical reaction. This happened to me that very evening. From the moment she began to speak, I was overcome with emotion and a strong conviction that this was an important moment. This was the mentor I needed. This same phenomenon still happens every time I hear her speak about finding your purpose in life.

Within the pages of this book—Life Outside the Box — are the stories of just ten of the many individuals whose journeys have touched my life. I love how each walks a path uniquely their own. I love that they define success in their own way and that all had twists and turns along the way to challenge them. The myriad of ways these challenges were met well up from the very core of who they are as human beings. No two paths are ever the same.

I have found my life's purpose and it is truly a journey of privilege. Every time I conduct an interview, whether with an elevator repairman on the subway in New York or with someone well-known, I am changed. This amazing path I am on has also brought the chance to mentor, to have a positive influence, and to help create a sense of community. To others I can only say, when you find your passion, embrace it. The journey will probably be an amazing roller coaster ride of highs and lows, but absolutely well worth the effort.

Ruthie Davis

"Throughout my career in footwear, what always inspires me and is the spirit of my work is pushing the limit, moving it forward, innovating—not only being current but knowing what's next—that's where I create. That's what excites me."

Entrepreneurship—starting your own company—has long been a goal for many in the business world. One development in this area that stands out is the increasing number of business women launching their own companies, a number that has doubled in the last ten years alone. And it's a trend that shows no signs of abating. Their track record overall has proven impressive and respected industry publications such as *Forbes* have taken notice.

One professional who offers an example of what these entrepreneurs bring to the table is luxury shoe designer Ruthie Davis—drive, determination, bold ideas, and an amazing work ethic. She has proven herself to have the Midas touch when working for other companies and brought that same business acumen to the table when launching her own international venture—a goal that has always been a part of her game plan. The Ruthie Davis brand is now an internationally recognized luxury label sold in thirty-five countries around the world.

Why shoes? Even her father knew this would most likely be her future when he viewed his daughter's teenage closet and pronounced that she "needed to marry rich or get into the shoe business." In looking back, it's obvious this interest began much earlier. The future shoe designer put on her first pair of red patent leather Mary Janes at the tender age of two and refused to take them off at bedtime. At age eleven, she was sporting a pair of baby platforms secretly given to her by her older sisters.

"I am the youngest of six kids and think one of the reasons I started liking high heels at a young age was because my older brothers and sisters were taller. When platforms came into vogue in the Seventies, my sisters bought me a pair of Korkys that were a good four inches high. I was eleven or twelve at the time. I would put them in my backpack and right before getting to school, I would change my shoes. My mother never knew."

Davis was born and raised in Connecticut surrounded by an extended family of writers, creators, journalists, and marketers, all of whom—especially her father—had a huge influence on her from an early age.

"Though it was my father who probably influenced me the most, much of his success was rooted in things he had learned from his father, my grandfather. My grandfather was the head of the Department of Journalism at Penn State. He wrote the first textbook on advertising in America and was inducted into the Advertising Hall of Fame. My dad used to reference my grandfather's teachings where he subscribed to always thinking in terms of *the hook*. 'What's the angle? What's the catch?' These teachings, along with hard work and perseverance, helped my father ascend the Stanley Tools Company, ultimately becoming its CEO. Similarly, I've carried the idea of the hook throughout my entire career. For everything I do, I ask, 'What is the theme? What is the main purpose? What's the reason for being?' Incorporating tried and true lessons handed down to me from the past has been one of my strengths."

Davis's Type A energy, focus, and drive were evident from an early age and she gave her full attention to every activity she embraced. While the standard childhood lemonade stand is well known, this creative young entrepreneur found a way to take it to the next level.

"I lived on the fifth hole of a golf course. This is where I set up a lemonade stand for the thirsty golfers ... BUT I made most of my profits selling used golf balls in bulk plastic bags that my dog, Springer Spaniel 'Woody' and I would find off course on the golf course. I would wash them and sell for like a dollar a bag."

Fashion and style also drew her, because they offered a chance to break new ground. By the time Davis hit prep school, a herd mentality drove what classmates wore. Not this teenager. Doing what had been done before never interested her and still doesn't today. Others began to sit up and take notice.

A talented and serious athlete, she was attracted to sports attire that was form fitting and enhanced the movement of the body. This did not in any way include the standard sports track suit.

"My wardrobe was very aerodynamic and sleek. I love the lines of the body and as an athlete, I had an appreciation for the human form and what it could do. When I got dressed for a ski race, I thought I was getting ready for a black tie event. My first love in fashion was for luxury sports collections like Chanel Sport and Prada Sport." Classmates loved the way these fashion-forward looks were put together and were soon seen offering hints of the same style.

After high school, it was off to study Liberal Arts at Bowdoin College, splitting her coursework between intellectual pursuits and artistic interests. English classes were balanced with art classes including drawing, photography, and watercolours, as creativity has always been a part of her nature.

"While growing up, I used to sketch shoes, buildings, and furniture. I continue to be inspired by architecture and furniture in my shoe designs today. I also expressed my creativity through my outfits."

Degree complete, with a love of sports and a major in English in hand, her first job was in sports journalism for ABC Sports at the Summer Olympics. Next up, Davis had been a summer intern at *The Hartford Courant* and was hopeful to be hired now full time. The interview happened, but the person in charge was dead set on finding someone with at least five years' serious experience, not a newbie writer just out of college.

But the word no just doesn't resonate with Davis when she has her eyes set on a goal.

She came back with an interesting counteroffer to write

one article for their review on a sports-related subject not previously covered. This was the Eighties—a time of Jane Fonda and the fitness craze. Aerobics were happening all over the Hartford area and Davis was well versed in the subject as she started and taught an aerobics program at Bowdoin. Intrigued, the paper said yes to an article about aerobics.

From that moment on, the finish line was clearly in sight. The job was hers to earn.

"When I went home, my dad asked me if I got the job and I said, 'Yes, sort of.' I still had my ID and keys to get into the building from my summer internship and the paper had a lot of extra desks and computers. So I started going to work every day."

After interviews, writes, re-writes, and polishing were done, the article was accepted for publication. While this one might have only paid $50, it led to regular assignments—first on the weekend sports beat and then travelling to cover college events. In her own words, "I basically turned 'no job' into a real job."

There are a few things about this experience that speak to Davis's strengths. First is the refusal to accept no. Another is the determination to not only do a good job when an opportunity opens, but to knock it out of the ballpark. The subject choice for that first article is also a perfect example of an ability she would become most known for over the years—to spot upcoming trends before anyone else and bring them to the table in an unexpected way. Covering aerobics as a sports columnist? Unheard of. Yet it landed her the job. Over time, this talent would earn her the title, "Cool Hunter." Trend-spotting is of course part instinct, but it's also the result of long hours spent doing extensive research.

That first article on aerobics would eventually lead Davis back to her childhood interest in entrepreneurship. After moving on to become a production assistant at ESPN (Entertainment and Sports Programming Network), she decided to open an on-trend fitness studio offering aerobics classes, personal trainers, etcetera. Business was quickly booming, especially once celebrity clients came calling.

This was only the opening note in her journey to launching an international company. To prepare for the future, more business savvy was in order. That meant heading back to school for an MBA. She chose the F.W. Olin Graduate School of Business at Babson College, because their Entrepreneurship and Marketing program is considered one of the best in the world.

The culmination of every MBA degree is the final project and her choice offered a glimpse of things to come. "I really became interested in footwear and ended up doing my final thesis on Rykä—a female-owned company producing athletic footwear for women. But I had no idea at the time I would end up in footwear down the road."

The next three jobs were important stops on her journey to becoming a luxury shoe designer, as each one offered the chance to gain invaluable knowledge and experience. The first door to open was at Reebok. Her combination of a sports background, sports writing, sports marketing, and an MBA proved a winning combination. Davis started out as a Product Manager. Several promotions followed that led her quickly up the ranks until she was running the Classics division. One important skill she brought to this leadership position came from her early involvement in athletics—the importance of creating and working with a solid, inspired team. Being in charge of a division also meant learning about and being involved in every step of the process from initial idea to retail sales.

"Each division—running, tennis, classics—was run as a separate entity with its own team. I was director of the classics division, so I would brief designers on what we needed, work closely with the merchandisers, and meet the people who were making the shoes. A shoe has to hit a price point, a shoe has to have a customer, and a shoe has to be marketed. I realized I was good at figuring out the link between all these moving parts and liked where they overlapped—design and marketing, sales and production, sales and marketing. That's where you learn to be a good designer."

To be truly knowledgeable about production meant being intimately familiar with the factories in China where they built the shoes. Looking back, Davis describes travelling to the factories in Asia as going to "shoe boot camp." This was twenty years ago and things were very different back then.

"The companies would send me to China, and we would go to the factories every day. We were intimately involved in the shoes and the process. I got down to the brass tacks of learning how to make shoes. In the factory, I was exposed to all the components and I learned how to put a shoe together. I really gained a lot of respect for the workmanship and the process."

During her time at Reebok, it became apparent that Davis had real talent for shoe design. Many of the ideas she brought to the table went on to perform well in the retail market. This was the time the media first began to refer to Davis as the "Cool Hunter" in honour of her uncanny talent for trend-spotting and her keen understanding of how to work the hook. A good example of this was her decision to use military dog tags to brand Reebok's classic runner.

"I realized a lot of design is, 'What's the hook?' I would take a trend and bring it to design. Dog tag collars were really big trend in the Nineties—a big look that everyone was wearing. So I did it on the Reebok Classic sneaker—a white leather jogger. There is a window on the side that says Reebok and has the British flag. My idea was to put an old metal dog tag imprinted with the Reebok logo in that same window. The shoe sold through the roof. I didn't reinvent the wheel; I didn't reinvent the shoe; I just put the sizzle on the steak."

After a proven track record of spotting and cashing in on trends, she began receiving numerous offers. Eventually, Davis accepted a position with UGG in Santa Barbara—a brand of casual, comfortable sheepskin boots originally from Australia. Still in its infancy, UGG offered her a more entrepreneurial type experience than the $700-million-a-year Reebok business. She would have more influence and leeway on the design and marketing of the product. Plus, it would be a great testing ground for some of her ideas.

What at first seemed like an odd pairing turned out to be a very successful one. Davis was able to quickly assimilate her East Coast business training and acumen into a laid-back West Coast company. This often involved not only working around the schedules of avid surfers, but also introducing new strategies. For instance, UGG had never had a marketing budget. Davis started by creating one, along with a business plan. She hired a product placement company to put UGG boots on celebrities including Brooke Shields, Pamela Anderson, and Kate Hudson. She hired a PR firm to get the brand exposure in magazines. And when it came to design, Davis knew it was all about creating the hook that would draw the public's eye.

"I took that sheepskin boot and made it more appealing by exposing the sheepskin on the outside of the boot—because that says luxury. I also created a lugged sole to make it seem more weatherproof for those on the East Coast. It was basically dialing up the product to fit the new luxury and fashion focused marketing positioning."

It took three years for all the changes to bear fruit and then UGG officially exploded as a hot new trend. Tommy Hilfiger took notice.

Although Davis enjoyed the wonderful climate and outdoor lifestyle of the West Coast, she knew she needed more grit in her life—a little more edge, a few rainy days. The designer has always wanted to work for a big fashion house. Tommy Hilfiger offered to move her back to New

York and again be in charge of footwear design and marketing. It was an offer and experience she couldn't refuse.

"Wherever I have worked, I try to do something that hasn't been done before. A lot of the girls wearing the Hilfiger label were really young and wanted to be a little hipper. The people at Tommy Hilfiger corporate wanted to go a little more conservative. I got around it by launching Tommy Girl Shoes, a younger division. I took the classic Hilfiger shoe and made it a little more fashionable, a little more trendy, a little more what the customer wanted."

After working with Reebok, UGG, and Tommy Hilfiger, it was time to execute a concept Davis had for her own luxury brand, which she describes as, "Imagine if … a Manolo Blahnik and a Nike had a baby." Impassioned by this hook, Davis left Tommy Hilfiger to work feverishly for a launch in 2006.

"I didn't spend a lot of time talking about what I was going to do. I just built the shoes. Playing off my love of futuristic and modern sports shoes, I created a wedge made out of titanium. It was very techie, like Mac's PowerBook G4. Then there were these really cool graphite heels. I don't have the energy to do something that has been done already. From the very first collection, people were drawn to my shoes because they are unique. For the launch, I chose a gallery in West Chelsea where we hung all the shoes as though they were art. At that point, rather than worrying about who was going to buy my shoes, I just wanted to see something tangible."

Despite all her time in the shoe industry, Davis had little

experience in how to market high-end luxury. There was no obvious road map to follow and while she knew the luxury accounts she wanted to sell it to, the designer wasn't sure how to reach them. But she had done her homework and knew how to use her dad's all-important hook to best advantage. Davis hired a PR company. She sent packets with photos and a cover letter to people; she placed samples in beautiful little bags and took them on cold calls; and she even loitered in stores befriending the sales clerks until the manager came in. Along the way, a deep conviction that the business was going to be a success carried her through the initial stages. Doubt didn't enter the picture.

"To be honest, there never was a light-bulb moment where I thought, 'This will be a success.' I just had faith that my years of experience in the industry, my commitment to work very hard, and my willingness to learn and grow from my mistakes all gave me a good chance to make it work. My confidence comes from the fact that I am a woman. I know what women want on their feet. This gives me great trust in my design instincts."

Davis's hard work quickly paid off when quality fashion magazines including *Elle* and *Women's Wear Daily* published photo editorials that included her shoe line.

"I caught the attention of those magazines from the very first collection because people are always looking to write about something different, something special."

Celebrity sightings soon followed. Garnering a client list that included Hollywood stars such as Beyoncé, Lady Gaga, Sofia Vergara, and Katy Perry meant an explosion of interest that quickly landed her designs on the red carpet and on the runway in fashion weeks. Her title soon changed from the Cool Hunter to Celebrity Shoe Designer, Ruthie Davis. That innate ability to offer new ideas created an unstoppable upward momentum.

There are several examples of how Ruthie Davis Shoes took a known element and found a way to make it new and exciting. For example, the use of metal studs as embellishment on high-end heels. Yes, studs on chunky boots and edgy clothing had been a part of the Goth counterculture for a long time, but it was a totally new element on luxury shoes. In addition, her use of the studs was unique as she clustered the studs on the heel counter of the shoe. She did this so that they didn't stick out on the sides or front of the shoe. By being clustered on the heel, they gave a more elegant, subtle, yet still cool pop of edgy detail. In addition, she created a stud that actually could screw on and off the shoe. This cluster of studs on the heel was soon copied by many high-end brands.

Then there was the use of neon colours. They had been a hot trend in athletic runners, but definitely hit a new and exciting note when seen in a super-high-end luxury stiletto heel. Celebrity sightings abounded. Competitors quickly tried to cash in on the new trend. No worries for the Cool Hunter as there are always new ideas waiting to be found.

Success has brought wider opportunities, with international travel being one of the biggest. For Davis, the standard vacation lying on the beach or touring historic sites is one she would love to embrace, but it just isn't what excites her. Taking trips to international destinations means opening her eyes to all the interesting ideas available. It is about seeing what's happening in other cultures and it is best done alone so there is complete freedom to explore.

"As part of my job, I try to go to as many fashion weeks as I can and I tie it into going to visit my factories and my showroom in Italy. I make sure to find time to visit the Centro to go to the stores and see what people are wearing. That's my favourite travelling—to be a fly on the wall observing. To be a good designer, especially if you're doing global fashions, you have to really understand the different consumers and what they're looking for."

Being involved in high profile fashion weeks is important for any luxury brand and Ruthie Davis Shoes have been on the runway since day one. The designer has collaborated in numerous shows including ones featuring designs by Duckie Brown, Katie Gallagher, Dennis Basso, and David Meister. Being in the front row watching her designs strut by is like watching her dreams come true.

Davis also uses television to increase brand awareness. "TV work has always been a part of my thing, and it gets back to my family of journalists, writers, and communicators. I like to communicate. I like to talk live. I like to talk about what I'm doing, so TV is a perfect medium for me."

The designer's résumé now includes Bloomberg Television, Fox 5, NBC, Bravo, and E! to name just a few. She also maintains a YouTube site offering a large selection of videos.

After eight years in the industry—twenty-four

collections—how does Davis approach inspiration each season? A multitasker at heart, the designer often uses her daily run to seek out new ideas. Anything can provide that initial spark. A street scene, the shape of a building, a passing car, a bit of graffiti, a spot of colour, a pedestrian's personal style—the possibilities are endless. Back in the studio, Davis immediately jots down notes and creates sketches. Inspiration also heralds back to her athletic roots and early fashion sense. It embraces confident women everywhere. The designer's ultimate muse is a James Bond girl in a one-piece ski suit, swooshing down the mountain.

"Confident, Glam, Fun" are three words that encapsulate Davis's entrepreneurial style as well as her brand. "Confident" refers to aggressively going after her dreams—a strong woman driven to reach new heights. "Glam" is the high style element the brand brings into a woman's life. It is okay to be strong and celebrate being a stylish woman. The two are not exclusive. Last of all is "Fun." Despite her incredible work ethic, the designer truly is doing what she loves—running her own label, putting in long hours, constant travelling, and interviews. They are what make life interesting and she brings this joy to her design work.

"At the end of the day, I don't take myself too seriously. I want to have fun. And fashion should be fun. Some people make fashion too intense. I love it when I see people look at my shoes and smile."

With success comes the ability to influence others, offer guidance to those just starting out, and affect change. Davis fully embraces being a role model and mentor, especially when it comes to young women wanting to enter the business world. Contacts through email alone can be overwhelming. Invitations to speak are numerous and offer a wide variety of ways to make a difference. If at all possible, she answers yes.

"I continue to mentor whenever opportunities come about. There's always something. Students from Babson that want to go into fashion contact me. I give them fifteen-minute phone interviews and advice. I do blog interviews and speak at high schools, colleges, and women's conferences. It's an ongoing thing. I usually don't say no if someone asks me to do something that will mentor others."

Affecting change also means being a part of charity efforts and the Ruthie Davis label has been involved in many such efforts over the last eight years. The most recent was in early 2014. An opportunity arose to collaborate with menswear designer John Bartlett. Together they created a limited edition collection of "cruelty-free" vegan shoes. Bartlett designed the signature "Tiny Tim" print, a colourful tribute to his much loved, three-legged pit bull who passed away in 2010. Davis applied her talents to building the three shoes—a high-heeled pump, a unisex high-top sneaker with spikes, and a unisex running shoe—that sported a canvas Tiny Tim print cover and 100 percent vegan soles. Ten percent of all sales were donated to Bartlett's Tiny Tim Rescue Fund, which provides funds to organizations that treat and find homes for animals in shelters.

Success for this entrepreneur is a journey that starts with

an idea. Then she develops a plan and works very hard to make it a reality. The reward is the moment it all comes together and the goal is reached. When it comes to design, this success is intimately tied to her customers. She has a vision for a new shoe, she creates a design, she makes a trip to Italy to put it into production, and finally the shoe hits the market. For Davis, this is the crucial moment.

"If the customer puts it on and says it's a fabulous shoe and it sells out, that's success for me."

When it comes to the brand, however, she has set the bar much higher. The goal is for her company to thrive and reach a brand recognition where it is a global household name. The plan is in place, the hard work is being done— it's only time before she reaches her goal. And Davis fully recognizes part of achieving her goals is the importance of working with a talented team.

"The most important element to any entrepreneur's success, especially mine, is putting together a good team. None of this can be achieved without the help of others. I have tried my best to team up with people who have complementary skills and talents to mine and encourage everyone on the Ruthie Davis team that my dreams are now their dreams too. Working as a cohesive unit is critical to bringing ideas from conception to the market. I have been very fortunate when it comes to building a great team."

While Davis's ambition has brought great recognition and achievements, it also has taken up most of her time and attention. She is the first to admit her professional and personal lives are closely intertwined. The designer loves her work, the long days, the jet-setting lifestyle, and the amazing people she works with. But she also values her personal life and has found a way for the two to thrive. After all, she needs moments away from the craziness.

First is her wonderful husband, Innes, who is fully supportive of the passion she holds for her company and the many hours she puts in. She offers the same in return. They offer each other the freedom to live without constraints. But he lures her away from the city some weekends and that change has proven to be a great one. "Recently, I've been spending time at this little house we have in Philly, fixing it up, working in the garden, and doing typical weekend chores and activities. One can often get lost in the demands of work and forget there other important things in life to be experienced. The weekends in Philly help me balance my life, and this in turn makes me a better designer. I'm trying to make more time for those weekends—to be with my husband and my dogs, Desert and River, and be away from fashion."

Another chance to step away from work came when she entered the New York City Marathon in November 2013. Type A down to her very core, Davis again put her eyes on the prize and committed fully to training hard. It was a challenge to be the best she could be and this goal was realized when she finished with the same time as when she had run the race in her twenties.

One of the highest moments in her career to date—both as an entrepreneur and a designer—came in April 2014 at the Grand Hyatt in New York City. It was here that the

American Apparel and Footwear Association (AAFA) held their annual American Image Awards to recognize outstanding achievements within the US Apparel and footwear industry. The designer received the AAFA Footwear Designer of the Year Award. Past recipients of awards at this event include notables such as John Bartlett, Badgley Mischka, Diane von Furstenberg, and Oscar de la Renta, so this was an overwhelming affirmation for Davis.

This was soon followed by an even greater honour when Davis was admitted as a member to the CFDA (Council of Fashion Designers of America)—the most prestigious fashion group in the country. Its ranks include the likes of Calvin Klein, Perry Ellis, Halston, Ralph Lauren, Donna Karan, Tommy Hilfiger, Carolina Herrera, Kenneth Cole, Oscar de la Renta, and Marc Jacobs. Membership in the CFDA is the brass ring for any American Fashion Designer.

Davis is now not only a leading independent designer internationally, but one of only a few female luxury shoe designers in America. The Ruthie Davis label has amassed over a hundred accounts and is sold in thirty-five countries around the world. The brand is leading the trends and bringing new energy and innovation to the industry.

The designer was overwhelmed with emotion the evening of the AAFA awards. Her acceptance speech offered thanks to her parents who encouraged her to think big and to know that anything was possible; to the exceptional team she works with side-by-side in a labour of love; to her husband Innes who always believes in her and offers her the best advice and consult—even at 11:00 a.m. Italy time, 5:00 a.m. New York time; and to her many industry friends who have supported her journey. But it ended with a special thanks to those who truly inspire her—the women who wear her shoes.

"I love designing shoes—and I always dreamed of building a brand with a strong DNA and identity. When people tell me they can recognize a Ruthie Davis shoe, that is the ultimate compliment. But I never lose sight that the purpose of my work, the design of a woman's shoe, is to celebrate how exquisite she is: modern, confident, sexy, and proud. As a woman designing for women, I know what it is to put on a pair of shoes and to feel transformed. To all of the women out there who I am honored to call my 'Ruthie Girls,' my ultimate gratitude is to you. Thank you for giving my vision a presence and a purpose. You are my forever inspiration and the true measure of my achievement."

Katherine Soucie

"I have always believed that fashion is art. Our clothing is the first thing others see. It is within this that one's sense of individuality and creativity is expressed. Having studied both fashion and textiles has allowed me to create opportunities with my work that challenge and develop conversations around what art and fashion are."

An intricate part of any culture's history can be found in the way textiles have been used—spiritual worship, preparing the dead, defining status, decorating homes, and sometimes just providing much-needed warmth for survival. No one knows exactly when the first textiles were created, but a study of surviving artifacts opens a window into the world they were part of. Today the term commonly brings two uses to mind. The first is the clothing that we use to express our individuality—often driven by the industry standard of two seasons a year, a constantly changing style, and mass production. The second is linens—curtains, sheets, duvet covers, towels, wall hangings, and area rugs—used to create an ambiance unique to our home environment. But if you look a bit deeper, there is so much more that textiles have to offer.

Textiles have become a lightning rod for those who support the Eco Fashion and Slow Fashion Movements.

Eco fashions strive to offer a change in the way clothing is currently manufactured. The focus is on production methods, fabrics, and dyes that are less damaging to the environment, as well as creating a healthier work environment for industry employees. The Slow Fashion movement came about as consumers began to recognize that creating garments worn for only one season and passé the next is just not sustainable. There is a slow but steady return to the idea that purchasing unique, quality pieces that will be an intricate part of your wardrobe for years to come is a better choice than poorly made seasonal offerings that are quickly disposed of. Upcycling of used clothing and linens has created a whole new generation of designers offering one-of-a-kind garments inspired by vintage materials.

Then there is textile art. Galleries increasingly feature installations from artists who choose textiles as their creative medium. Katherine Soucie embraces all three worlds: art, fashion, and sustainability. Her label—Sans Soucie— means "without a care."

Artists seem to be born with a different way of looking at the world—it's evident from day one—and Soucie is no exception. Raised in Southern Ontario, the future designer was challenged as the youngest child to find a way to express her individuality. Her starting point was being the youngest of five girls who accumulated a never-ending pile of fashion magazines and hand-me-downs. Add in a mixed cultural heritage—British, French Canadian, Métis, German, Seneca, and Oneida—and the foundation was laid. Creating her own unique, personal expression that also honoured her heritage was a challenge quickly accepted. It was all about transformation.

Music was another important influence that began at a very early age.

"My first memory was of sitting down at a piano at age three and playing a song I had been singing earlier that day. It was easy for me to express myself through music, something that has carried on through my adult life. Music is a deeply personal experience that inspires me and it's a huge contributor to my creative process as an artist."

Hints of a budding entrepreneurial spirit were also apparent early on. By the age of four, she was selling produce from her parents' garden—something she's not sure they ever figured out. That was followed by bake sales, lemonade stands and a paper route.

By the age of five, Soucie was completely in charge of her wardrobe. At the age of eight—the 1980s—the future designer began to be more expressive in the way she dressed. There was always that pile of fashion magazines ready to open a window on what was happening in the world at large, but her sisters' hand-me-down garments offered their own spark of inspiration.

"I always had hand-me-downs, but I began to explore various ways to wear the same garment. I was inspired by old Hollywood film stars—one day it was Marilyn Monroe. I decided to take a black sweater dress and wear it on a hot summer day in a reconfigured manner. I wore it as a strapless dress with the sleeves tied in a bow around my flat chest. I remember feeling beautiful and feminine.

Then I jumped on my BMX bike and went to play with my friends. This was the beginning of a relationship with clothing as a form of my identity—culturally, socially, and politically—and I began to explore making and remaking vintage clothing."

Another important influence appeared during summers camping with her family at the Pinery Provincial Park near Lake Huron. It was here she was introduced to recycling and became more mindful of how to care for the natural environment—only bring essentials and produce little to no waste. Days were spent roaming the lakefront, beaches, hiking trails, and paths collecting all kinds of garbage and disposing of it. Cleaning up after teenage parties meant dealing with cigarette butts, bottles, bottle caps, and cans carelessly left behind.

"I became an activist in the Park's recycling program and was recognized with an award in their Friends of the Environment Program. This experience helped me choose to actively participate and educate others on waste in the natural environment."

By high school, Soucie already knew that fashion design would be in her future. The local high school fortunately had a great Home Economics program that taught not only sewing skills, but also pattern drafting. One night the seventeen-year-old was hand sewing details on a final project that was late—again—and left her large needle in a vintage wicker and upholstery reading chair. In a rush the next morning to get ready for school, she was startled by a loud plop. Lo and behold, there was now a 3.5" darning needle sticking out of her foot. Pulling on it only removed about half, so she was off to the emergency department. The needle was wedged securely into the heel's cartilage and an operation was needed to remove it. A week passed before the small hospital could schedule the surgery. Her foot swelled up like a balloon, but she took the whole experience in stride.

"I thought to myself, who does this happen to? If I have to die for my craft and my love of all things fashion, then so be it. It became a part of my pilgrimage to the trade. After the surgery they gave me the piece of needle, which I still have to this day. I like to think this experience taught me to never forget my passion and path in life—that no obstacle will deter me from where I should be."

After high school, Soucie headed off to Fanshawe College to study fashion design. The program proved a disappointment, as coursework was often a repetition of work already completed in high school. But Soucie persevered. One high point was her sewing instructor.

"I was a bit of troublemaker and socialite, hanging out with a lot of musicians. I felt I wasn't being challenged. She was a real hard-ass teacher and didn't like anyone, but she pushed me hard and really helped me develop my sewing skills."

Soucie's first year design collection—couture dresses created from recycled duct tape and vintage broadcloth—was awarded first place and recognized as the Most Innovative and Outrageous Collection in the school's 1997 show. The designer knew she was on to something. It was time to look into other schools. Classes at George Brown College came first, followed by further studies at Ryerson University. Education would be a constant theme in years to come, with the designer sometimes in the role of student and other times in the role of educator teaching textile science and surface design.

A move to British Columbia would provide one of those all-important defining moments. It all began with a decision to enter the Textile Arts program at Capilano University in North Vancouver. Studying textiles is important to anyone hoping to pursue a career in fashion design. Just like an architect, a fashion designer has to understand the material they're working with before they can start building a structure. A poor understanding of a fabric's unique characteristics often leads to disastrous results.

Capilano's Textile Arts program allowed Soucie to explore her interest in non-traditional textiles. Recycled materials including coffee filters, dryer sheets, and nylon stockings were the raw materials that, through experimentation, she transformed into wearable garments.

"I grew up in the Eighties when there were great campaigns to get us to recycle and that has always stuck with me. I didn't want to work in an industry that was wasteful. It became apparent to me there was an overabundance of non-functional textiles in our world that needed to be made functional."

The fashion industry as it currently stands creates a huge amount of waste. Hosiery waste in particular stands out.

Any product not up to standards is either sold off through a budget liquidator such as a dollar store, or sent to the dump where it becomes a permanent resident. It doesn't decompose. What could be done with this fairly fragile product to give it a new life?

Soucie was interested in working with knits, so she was drawn to find a solution. First she developed a method that enabled her to stabilize the nylons and structurally change the surface of the material. The next step was exploring how to permanently dye the product in a way that had the least environmental impact. This included more natural avenues such as exposing the fabric to rust as well as to more ecofriendly commercial products and surface design applications. From this point on, she turned her creative focus to what silhouettes would best showcase the fabric's unique characteristics. Creating your own textile right down to the palette is the Holy Grail for anyone creating fashion and the designer was excited about the fabric's potential.

"This gave me complete control of the entire process and allowed me the opportunity to develop something that is uniquely Canadian from fabric to finished product."

One of her textile teachers was intrigued and encouraged her to pursue this direction even further. Soucie's 2003 grad project featured a collection of garments created from this unique textile called *The Polymer Series*. This was the moment when something that began as a class project changed into the foundation on which she would build her own label. *The Polymer Series* was awarded two scholarships that funded the launch of Sans Soucie, along with an offer to join an exhibit at the Pendulum Gallery in Vancouver.

"At that point I already had five years of post-secondary education and was literally thrown to the lions. Circle Craft was celebrating their thirty-year anniversary at the gallery and I was the first scholarship recipient. There I was with what I thought was a silly little concept and it sold out opening night. It's one thing to have a student show where your work sells, but it was a big deal to be asked to exhibit in a gallery, have the curator tell you your items have all sold, and be asked if you can bring in more work. I had to go back to work the next day and start from scratch. Those new pieces sold as well."

Five years later, she found out one of her regular clients had actually purchased one of those first dresses that very night.

Right from the beginning, Soucie knew she wanted to be a couturier and be as environmentally friendly as possible. Industry notions of production methods and schedules were discarded first. Each new Sans Soucie collection is released as an art series of couture garments that have a given inspiration. Three new collection launches a year is the average, but the timing varies according to when the new work is ready.

Inspiration comes from a wide variety of sources. The beauty found in decay, renewal, and the cyclical nature of life has always held a special attraction for her. The design-er regularly incorporates these elements in several ways including her use of rust in the dying process. Victorian lace and architecture; the Edwardian "Belle Époque" period when women began to remove their corsets and wear simpler clothing; and even the small structures seen through the lens of a microscope have held sway in other years. Palettes change to reflect the different inspirations—one series in black and white (during a time of inner turmoil), another in pastels, and yet another offering vivid splashes of bright colours. Layering of different shades and themes during the silk-screening process adds an interesting textural element to the completed garment.

The production process is time consuming—a full two weeks from start to finish just to complete one piece. A batch of raw, pre-consumer waste nylon hosiery arrives from mills based in Montreal and North Carolina. The pantyhose is stabilized through a lengthy process that begins with cleaning. From here they are dyed, cut open to create a flat strip of cloth, silk-screened with a pattern unique to the current series, air cured, and then colours are heat set. Soucie owns dress forms in a wide size range to suit her diverse clientele. Each garment is created by the designer personally, one at a time, right on the dress form using only pins, a pair of scissors, and an unfailing intuition.

"I start by sectioning the fabric, then draping, and cutting. I use one or two pins and that's it. Then I do all the finishing. The sewing doesn't take me long and I find it very meditative, but the process to get it all done is very time-consuming."

There are some basic principles to guide her, but the combination of colours and shapes comes together in a truly organic way. In the end, they are fabric sculptures—wearable works of art. Each is one-of-a-kind and the uniqueness of this process makes her line instantly recognizable.

What loyal clients love about San Soucie garments is they are defined by a person's shape. They invite a person to embody an experience with their clothing and are designed to transform over time as they continue to be worn. This symbiotic process creates a unique relationship between the garment and wearer that speaks to an authentic expression of the owner's identity, culture, and style. On a hanger the garment can be fairly non-descript, only coming to life when worn. Its ultimate shape is defined by a woman's unique silhouette, so an outfit will never look exactly the same when worn by two different clients. And being rail thin is not an asset. These clothes celebrate a body's curves.

Equally appealing is the fact they are oh-so-easy to care for. The garments can be run through the washer and dryer, stuffed in a suitcase for travel, and never need ironing. The San Soucie brand is worn by clients ranging in age from twenty-five to seventy-five and offered in sizes four to sixteen. Clients include writers, dancers, artists, designers, musicians, business women, mothers, teachers, lawyers, VIPs from several industries, and celebrities such as Halle Berry and Norah Jones.

Time away from production is important to avoid burnout. Invitations to create art installations offer the designer new challenges and a chance to step outside her daily routine. Here Soucie can use her unique medium to express ideas and make social comment. Some installations are solo exhibitions; others are welcome collaborations.

"I love the collaborative process. It allows me to develop truly exceptional pieces."

All along the way, public recognition has provided continuing affirmation that Soucie's work is important. Her résumé is filled with a long list of awards including the 2006 British Columbia Creative Achievement Award, the 2007 Niche Award, the 2008 International Design Green Award; with numerous international art installations, grants, and workshops; with runway shows at fashion weeks; with inclusion of eight of her designs in a coffee table book titled *1,000 Artisan Textiles: Contemporary Fiber Art, Quilts, and Wearables* by Gina M. Brown and Sandra Salamony, 2010; and with invitations to show at Esthetics in London, England and to exhibit in Guangzhou, China at the National Silk Museum during the ninth World Shibori Network Symposium in 2014.

Every artist working with a specific medium has to find a way to continue to grow or their work can become stagnant. Since that first successful show in 2003, Soucie has continued to expand her work as an artist, designer, and educator. It is a never-ending journey of evolution—exploring new ideas, incorporating elements of interest, and mentoring others.

"I believe in giving back. I give as much as I take. It comes back down to this: there needs to be a balance in the industry and I want to help create it; to inspire other designers to really think about what they're doing in their practices." Education has always held an important role in her journey and the designer fully admits, "I am a bit of an education junkie."

In 2007, this educational bent led to her entering the Emily Carr University of Art + Design where she completed a Master's Degree in Textiles. Capilano University had developed a relationship with Emily Carr that helped open the door, but there was much to do to make her degree a reality. The university did not currently have a set Master's program in Textiles.

"I felt it was the right opportunity for me to go into an institution where there is such a strong interest in textiles, but no particular curriculum established. Most of my work was in the Industrial Design department, but not much in the Visual Arts."

Soucie enjoyed heading back to school and was given a great deal of freedom in developing the curriculum and the direction of her research. She was asked to become one of the school's partners, working in the lab on new projects alongside students, as well as developing community workshops to be held at the lululemon lab—a place where loyal customers of the brand can watch designers create clothing from inception to hanger.

Soucie used her studies at Emily Carr to expand upon the eight-plus years of research and development she had dedicated to her signature hosiery textile process.

"I was really interested in making creative conversation

around mass production, how that fits in our society today, the people that still embrace it, and those who are abandoning it. I had a pretty free range to do what I wanted. There was a lot of studio time and I was working mostly with embroidery and print making."

A commercial embroidery machine in the studio offered her the chance to explore how to develop what is normally a surface decoration into a construction technique she calls "visual mending." In visual mending, the surface of the cloth is constructed—or reconstructed—to create a new fabric with its own unique identity. It is completely original and one of a kind. Every new collection embodies elements of the designer's current focus, so it was no surprise to see textural embroidery becoming an intricate part of her next series—an element still visible in her work today.

The artist's research into this area of study is closely linked to her thoughts on the current state of the textile and garment industry, exposing and revealing what is often hidden from view. With the emergence of mass production, the connections among culture, production, and beauty have been lost. Soucie firmly believes that hand applications such as embroidery can coexist in harmony with modern industrial practices. Handcraft techniques, obsolete sewing and textile machinery, and digital textile equipment combined with a zero-waste philosophy all co-exist in her studio. This hybrid production style allows for exciting new discoveries that challenge the fashion industry's current methods.

Due to the lengthy amount of time it takes to produce a Sans Soucie original textile or garment, the artist often develops intimate relationships with her tools and equipment. As much of her equipment is obsolete and discarded, she began to refer to them by dinosaur-inspired names. Each has its own story. While working in the WIPlab (the lab for wearables and interactive products) at Emily Carr University, the studio that houses the large industrial embroidery machine, she decided one day that the perfect name for her faithful companion was *T. rex*.

"I was listening a lot to music while I worked, and then out of the blue looked at the machine and thought to myself …WOW! This machine really looks like a *T. rex*! It's big, powerful, intimidating, and has over sixteen needles that could take my hand out with one chomp. Yet those needles were also very fragile, like the hands of the *T. rex*. In my opinion the small hands are what made the beast obsolete as the dinosaur couldn't fight well. Well, for this machine, it was also its weak point and held up production many, completely frustrating times."

Before *T. rex* came along, Soucie had already named other machines that are a part of her fleet. Two of the most important are Meryl, the faithful Merrow sewing machine she uses to reconstruct the strips of hosiery into new cloth. Then there is Kenny the Kansai, a broken Japanese cover-stitch machine (serger) she uses as a drawing machine to embroider. The identity her tools possess are integral to the personality and environment she creates while working.

"These tools do a majority of the hard work. I am there

to assist, interrupt, and redirect when needed. It's a collaborative process and we have fun. Yes, they are inanimate objects to the average person, but without them I could not do what I do. Their raisons d'être are apparent. Their roles assist in the transformation of the materials in a way that breaks a pattern in how we view industrial tools."

The artist also works with new technology, but is frustrated by the planned obsolescence inherent in the equipment's design. Most industrial machines are designed and produced with the intention they be used for one application only. While this is useful within the chain of larger production, for Soucie their purpose embraces so much more. For her, the relationship between artist and instrument is an intimate journey of discovery. Her machines are taken out of retirement and allowed to find a new purpose.

"I explore with my tools in a way that allows them to find a sense of rhythm and voice after being retired from service so to speak. I believe this. Kind of like when someone retires and finally has the time to enjoy what they really love to do. There is something to be said about the relationship between an artist and her tools."

While enrolled at Emily Carr, the designer travelled to San Francisco to attend a workshop on Subtraction Cutting being run by UK designer Julian Roberts. In 1998, Roberts gained international recognition when he developed a revolutionary way to approach drafting. Rather than creating a pattern to reproduce a specific design, the design is created in response to the pattern. Negative spaces are cut away to create the hollow within the garment where the body resides. The concept can be difficult to explain, but in a workshop, the possibilities become crystal clear. Subtraction Cutting (SubCut) offers a more organic way of approaching design, and the garments produced are often unexpected. The concept exploded onto the scene with lectures and workshops held worldwide—Canada, Mexico, Australia, US, Russia, New Zealand, Spain, Portugal, Denmark, Sweden, China, Nigeria, Chile, Colombia, Argentina, and France.

Soucie's way of producing garments was already very organic, so the process of working with hollow spaces intrigued her. This was a three-day intensive that not only inspired her, but changed her life. Roberts was also intrigued by the rust-dyed fabric Soucie brought to work with as well as the process used to produce it. A conversation began—colleagues sharing ideas—that would end up benefitting both and influencing Soucie's next series.

"After working with him in San Francisco, I returned to Vancouver to begin a new body of work in the research lab at Emily Carr University. I began to explore using his cutting technique with my textile process and the digital embroidery. I constructed the hosiery cloth with the embroidery and hosiery hemming machine prior to exposing it to his emergent garment-cutting process. The first works I produced were five garments I exhibited under the title, *Vanitas*. This series of couture garments challenged the notion of handmade in the digital age and was shown in Canada, the United States, and the UK."

Images of these five garments were sent to Roberts,

who was so impressed he extended an invitation for the designer to join him on his tour in the US and Canada. The *Vanitas* garments were shown right alongside Robert's own work at events hosted by prominent design universities. There were discussions and workshops with students who were invited to exhibit their own work beside Robert's and Soucie's. A year later an email arrived from Roberts asking if she could post pictures of some of her SubCut garments and patterns on his Facebook page and also if he could include her in an upcoming book—*Free Cutting*.

To receive affirmation from the public is a wonderful reward, but there is something special when an artist's work is recognized by a colleague they admire. The most exciting moments in her life to date were the ongoing, inspiring conversations the two held.

"We are both designers who think and operate from a similar mindset and philosophy. We are both creative thinkers and educators in Fashion and Textiles who believe that fashion, art, design, and science are all interrelated. One does not exist without the other and we must encourage the making of mistakes in order to create new pathways in our work. I feel as if I met a soul mate in the creative realm. A true comrade. Someone who spoke the same language as me and someone who continues to inspire me with his words, thoughts, and ability to maintain his own path in the field of fashion."

In June 2013, Soucie travelled to the International Surface Design Association conference in San Antonio, Texas. The focus that year was Zero Waste Textile/Design/

Art Practices. Little did she realize an out-of-the-blue invitation to become a Visiting Professor in Textiles at the Welch School of Art and Design in Atlanta would come from a fellow attendee. The timing was not great, but the offer was too good to pass up.

"I was at a point in my career where I was no longer able to obtain hosiery resources in Canada. Since I work with mill waste and had received notification from the main mill I had worked with over the past ten years that their production would be decreasing and relocating to Asia, a lightbulb went off. I was knee-deep in trying to find a new resource for waste hosiery, and here I was invited to the Deep South where a history of textile production existed and mills remained. I have to admit I did not go to teach per se. I wanted to insert myself into this space with a history of production—to rediscover the remnants left behind."

Soucie lived on the border of two Atlanta neighbourhoods—Cabbagetown and Reynoldstown. The first was where the poor, white mill workers lived; the other, the first black neighbourhood established in the US after the civil war. The history of this area—the mills and racial unrest—still held an influence. Soucie initially looked into purchasing an abandoned mill to offer local production and consumption of textiles, but that was a dead end.

"Seeing the impact of how the labour and production of textiles had come to shape this geography made me realize this is not where I wanted to insert my vision. It was an environment that was clearly still suffering."

There was also an interesting twist—the main source of support for the mills that still exist are actually in China, Russia, and Eastern Europe. There, an emergent middle class have created a demand for garments featuring a *Made in the US* label, both for the quality and as a status symbol. North American designers are not the backbone of this industry. If not for the offshore buyers, these mills would close.

The year Soucie spent in Atlanta was an eye-opener on many fronts. It also helped clarify her vision of the industry. Mass production would not be going away, but current market practices were not sustainable. Balance was needed and the seeds of change were planted, nourished, and allowed to grow.

"I think the most important thing for me to recognize and accept is the aftermath suffered from a history of production and consumption. Rather than save or change it, insert a possibility that the handmade can coincide with mass production. We need to look toward trying to create opportunities where that can happen. To me that is sustainable."

While in Atlanta, a new opportunity arose, this time in New York City. From January through May 2015, Soucie will be a guest instructor at a textile school in Brooklyn. This coincides with her goal to have a showroom and artist studio in Vancouver where the main production will take place, as well as a showroom/studio in New York City for the brand's large number of Asian and US clients. This expansion, however, does not mean a change in volume. The time-consuming process to create a Sans Soucie garment will always limit production. These are art pieces—couture garments—to be valued for years to come.

To address the issue of sustainability, if a Sans Soucie piece begins to wear or no longer fits due to body changes, the customer can bring it back to have it repaired or used to create a new garment. The designer also believes in the concept of Zero Waste where nothing is ever thrown away. Whether it is a remnant from production or a garment beyond repair, everything finds a new purpose. The line now offers a wide range of accessories including armbands, cosmetic bags, stockings, leggings, hats, and blankets. Many of these offer an entry-level price point for a consumer on a more limited budget.

Throughout her entire life, Soucie has sought a path to live positively in this world as well as to look for solutions to the growing struggle for personal identity. Who are we? How do we express our individuality? What path is best to help create a better life for everyone in our community? Is it possible to live in a gentler way that consciously leaves a smaller footprint? At least some of the answers are found in being accountable for the work we do.

"I believe in creating work that not only represents the cyclical nature that the fashion industry naturally operates within, but also respects my philosophies toward design. I think my work educates people on the environment, yet it expresses a desire to communicate to the world the importance of individuality when it comes to how we dress and the value that comes along with owning articles of clothing that are investment pieces. There needs to be a balance in the industry. I want to contribute to a change in how we view clothing, how we choose to wear it, and how we choose to discard it."

Success has been a subject that Soucie has struggled with over the years. The common definition includes financial rewards and celebrity status. For this artist, success comes in many forms: meaningful work she is proud of, helping consumers find their identity through the clothing, accessories, and forms she creates, and being in a position of influence to change and alter the negative into the positive.

"I believe the hand has the ability to transform, not the machine. With negative forms of energy and production, things are not sustainable. Sustainability is about maintenance. This cannot happen without balance. My practice takes the negative [waste] and inserts applications through historical means employed by hand, resulting in a harmony in material and form. Giving new life or raisons d'être— reasons for being. That is not to say success does not reside in the works that are in progress, but it is a cycle that never ceases to end."

Soucie can be compared to a kaleidoscope that continues to offer us an ever-changing view. One aspect is her life-long desire to learn and grow. Another shows us a mentor and teacher ready to guide the next generation. Then there is the talented fashion designer who encourages personal identity. Next we see the artist within offering installations full of depth and meaning. Following comes her work as an eco-conscious producer concerned about zero waste.

Yet another highlights the activist with a deep concern for humanity who embraces social responsibility. The future will most likely continue to see Katherine Soucie exploring an ever more diverse number of interests, but in the end, all those pieces will again weave together in future projects to create a unified voice.

In her own words, "My best work is yet to come."

Geir Ness

"Imagine starting a business in a country in which you're not a citizen and have not mastered the language—a place where you have no family, money, or any contact to help get you started."

The world of perfume has exploded in recent years. It is a branding item for everyone from couture fashion houses to celebrities of all genres, with many offering several choices. Scents are embraced by both men and women—men often gravitating to muskier offerings, while women seem to embrace lighter mixes. It can be overwhelming to walk into a high-end department store with hundreds of enticing fragrances to choose from—all in elegantly designed bottles. For some customers, the attraction starts with the brand. For more knowledgeable clients, the choice is an exploration of finding that perfect, unique aroma to complement their personal style.

Throughout history, perfumes have held an important role in areas other than as a wardrobe accessory. At one time, they were used almost exclusively in religious rites by priests who offered these scents in worship to the gods and used them to anoint bodies being prepared for the next world. Fragrances were also embraced by society's elite as a sign of wealth and refinement.

Today, incense is still being burned on altars, but also as an aromatic in the home. Smudging with perfumes clears homes of spirits, and commercial buildings circulate well-chosen aromas to create a specific ambiance. But the largest use of scents today is in personal perfumes. It is estimated that by 2015 the fragrance industry will hit the thirty-three-billion-dollar mark globally, with women hands down its biggest customer. One perfumer who stands out in the industry for his truly unique marketing and business direction is Geir Ness.

Ness is a force of nature, full of boundless energy, endless passion, and tremendous focus. His presence fills the room. This is a man living his passion, who gives 110 percent to every single aspect of his life—the brand he loves, his very loyal clients, his own health, and his giving back through charity involvement. When looking back over his journey to success, what stands out is an unquestioning optimism—fear just doesn't seem to come into the equation. However, this optimism is backed up by sheer hard work. Even fifteen years after launching his fragrance, the perfumer still travels up to three hundred days a year promoting, meeting fans, being interviewed on TV, and raising money for worthy causes. Why? Because it's personal.

Ness was born in Oslo, Norway, into a family full of love but short on spending cash. The family of five—father, mother, and three active sons—lived in one unit of a four-plex. All three brothers shared the single bedroom, while his parents slept in the living room. Privacy was something you could only dream of. He remembers, "We didn't even have a bathroom in our unit. If you had to go in the middle of the night, you had to walk down two floors. There was no heat in the stairway and in winter it could be twenty below. Sometimes, the light wasn't working."

Although his home was humble, it was rich in all areas that mattered. The concept of being poor was foreign to Ness, because it was the same for everyone in the neighbourhood. There was always love and support from his parents, food on the table, a roof over their heads, and the beautiful countryside to enjoy.

"I grew up that way so I thought it was normal. You take care of yourself. You work hard."

To make up for the lack of room indoors, the family spent a lot of time outdoors. In the winter that meant cross-country and downhill skiing. His dad was an instructor and had Ness on the slopes before he could even walk. Then there was his father's cabin an hour outside Oslo where the family would spend two months every summer hiking, exploring nature, and enjoying all the local plants and wildflowers in bloom. This time in his youth would be pivotal in the development of what would become his passion—Laila Parfum.

Money was tight, so taking part in extra-curricular activities meant paying for everything yourself. Ness took his first job at the age of thirteen and was soon working three—delivering newspapers before school and on weekends, getting up at 3:30 in the morning to cook waffles at a cantina, and cleaning floors in offices. Paycheques went to cover the costs of participating in sports, which he loved, attending camp, and engaging in another growing passion—horseback riding. Saving money also became a habit early on and at the age of seventeen, he purchased his first condo.

His mother stressed it was important to care and respect for those less fortunate, and Ness took that to heart. One strong memory from his teens is of three years spent one-on-one with a disabled boy at the local equestrian centre.

"Once a week, the stables offered the opportunity for handicapped children to come and ride. I worked with one who had no muscle tone in his body. It was good for him to be on the horse. The last day his father gave me a gift—a silver letter opener—along with a sealed letter he had written for his son who could not speak. I was to use the gift to open the envelope. I felt so guilty, I cried all the way home. I said then that one day I wanted to do something again to give back and that's why I continue to be involved in charity work to this day."

Ness was twenty when a new life beckoned—the palm trees and beautiful beaches of Spain. The easiest way to get there was as a tour guide, but his résumé didn't include two of the most important qualifications—you had to be fluent in Spanish and familiar with the island of Mallorca. Never one to walk away from a challenge, and confident he could do the job, he decided to give it his best shot.

There was a long line of applicants already in line when he arrived—hundreds ahead of him all waiting to apply—but the interview went well. Then he caught a fortunate break. The person who was supposed to check his Spanish fluency had stepped out for a moment, so the dreaded test was waived. No one was more surprised than Ness when a job offer came through.

"I started to freak out as I had no clue what I was going to do when I arrived."

A couple of days later he was on a plane headed for Mallorca knowing only a few words of Spanish, almost nothing about the island, and feeling more than just a little nervous.

Two tour guides picked him up from the plane, gave him a uniform, and dropped him off at the hotel where he would be stationed. The tourists were from Scandinavia so it would be easy to answer their questions, but he had to deal with local Spanish-speaking people to rent cars, etcetera. Back then none spoke English. A family from Sweden was the first client to approach me that morning and Ness remembers the moment like it was yesterday.

"The dad tells me they want to go somewhere that's not overrun with tourists and asks for my recommendations. I answered that there were lots of options. As I was talking, I was reading upside down what it said about this area on the tourist map and repeating it back to them. The map listed a famous restaurant called Casa Gloria where the speciality is paella, so I told them to go there and also to visit the great beach in the area. Then I had to call for a rental car and pretend to speak Spanish."

Using a crib sheet of key Spanish words, he did his best to order a car, but had no idea what the person on the other end was saying in reply. In the end, the car fortunately arrived fifteen minutes later and his clients left, impressed.

A quick learner, Ness soon had a good enough grasp of the language to get by and a solid knowledge of Mallorca's tourist industry. Everything moved along smoothly for about three months until a phone call came from the head office asking him to come in right away. The boss wanted to speak with him. Assuming this was not good news—he figured he was going to be fired.

What came next was a total surprise. On entering the office, the secretary handed him a letter saying, "The boss wants you to read this." It was from that very first family. The letter was one of gratitude for the great service he'd provided and commented that they had never met a guide so knowledgeable. They mentioned visiting Casa Gloria three times and enthused about how wonderful the food was. Ness's boss threw him a set of keys and promoted him right then and there to a new position managing part of the island. With the new job came an apartment, a car, and thirty-five employees to supervise.

Mallorca offered an evening theatre for tourists. Stage had always been one of Ness's passions in high school, so it wasn't long before he began spending his evenings as the show's Master of Ceremonies. When parts in the cabaret opened up, he was quick to step in. His strong performances caught the eye of a Swedish producer who suggested studies in London, New York, or Los Angeles, but it took some time for the idea to take hold. Finally, he made the decision to give acting a try and a move to Los Angeles became the most important first step to achieving that goal.

"I wrote to several schools there including Stella Adler's and received a letter to come for an audition. I was twenty-five." Commitment made, audition booked, and plane ticket purchased, Ness told his parents he had been accepted as he didn't want them to worry. There was no room for any thoughts of failure. He would study acting in Los Angeles. It was as simple as that.

Ness was introduced to the seamy side of Los Angeles his first night.

"I rented a car, drove up to Hollywood to spend a couple of days before the audition, and figured I would just stay at a cheap hotel. The streets were full of nightclubs and hookers. I parked my car and booked a room only to find someone else was already staying in it. So I went back to the front desk, changed my room, and then walked out to see two big guys trying to break into my car. I hadn't locked it and everything I owned was in the trunk. I was scared, but I ran toward them and started to fight. Somehow, one fell and got hurt. Then I looked up the street and saw eight people coming toward me with chains, so I jumped in my car and took off. That was the start of my welcome to Hollywood. Sometimes, you do stupid things."

Still, when he called his mom later that evening, his only comment was that Los Angeles was amazing.

Even with little English vocabulary, Ness passed the audition and was accepted into acting school. His initial thought was that acting classes would get rid of his accent. That proved not to be the case. Adler wanted him to be true to who he is and encouraged him by saying, "Don't try to be American or anyone else. Just be who you are and you will be successful whether you want to keep acting or do something else. If you are just you, you'll be fine."

A few acting jobs began to roll in. One movie role he particularly enjoyed was playing the part of a vampire. "I love parts that are so far away from who I am." He had to reach deep inside to create the character. The scene played out on the Santa Monica Beach at night. First, the vampire danced with the actress. Then he bit her on the neck causing blood to flow. The intensity he brought to the performance ended up frightening the actress as well as the crew. They thought he would actually do it.

Roles were few and far between, so—as with most actors—money was tight. Side jobs as a seat filler for television shows helped bring in some extra cash. A modelling agency also signed the handsome Norwegian to work as an underwear model. Bits of money came in here and there, but the budding actor was always on the lookout for more work.

When a friend could not make his gig as a department store fragrance model, Ness was happy to step in, but the job only lasted five minutes! It is his nature to always give 110 percent and he followed his friend's instructions to the letter. "My friend said you just spray everyone that comes in and I thought he meant EXACTLY that. So when the door opened, I just ran up and sprayed and sprayed and sprayed." It wasn't long before the manager noticed the chaos. He quickly came over and fired the over-zealous employee.

True to form, it didn't take long for Ness to learn the ropes and become a regular fragrance model in several different department stores, at perfume launches, and at in-store events, especially in Nordstrom. Customers were drawn to the striking blond with an interesting accent and would often stop to talk. There was one question that arose time and time again that would end up providing the spark for what would become a four-year quest. "Doesn't Norway have its own fragrance?" The answer was no—a few oils, but no international fragrance. Ness was intrigued.

"I helped launched all these high-end fragrances—if Donna Karan had an opening for her new fragrance, I was a part of it—and started to learn more about the industry. After being asked that question so many times, I began to think there was a market for a Norwegian perfume."

A retired perfumer who had worked for several big brands was in Los Angeles at the time. Ness met him at a party and quickly asked his advice on how to create a fragrance. The answer was simple. "First you have to figure out what kind of scent you want and what kind of ingredients you like." Once that was clear, the perfumer was willing to help him out.

Memories of Ness's time spent outdoors as a child in Norway came to mind—long family hikes in the mountains surrounded by aromatic shrubs and wildflowers, their fragrances wafting on the breeze. It was time for a trip home to search for inspiration. While on vacation, he picked his favourite flowers and fresh herbs, and brought them back to the perfumer. It was time to get down to the hard work of formulating the perfect scent. He wanted to capture the beauty of Norway in a bottle.

The retired perfumer was a true gift. Today you would have to have money in hand and a company to back you to even get started, but it was different in the Nineties. He generously decided to help Ness simply because he liked him, so the research phase cost nothing. The perfumer smelled each of the samples and then listened to his client's vision.

"I don't want it strong and heavy. I want it very clean, light, and sporty. It also has to be created from the most natural ingredients possible so people who have allergies can wear it."

The perfumer headed back to New York City and then off to Europe. Every now and then a new sample would arrive in Los Angeles to be considered, but it never was just Ness's opinion that mattered. The fragrance model wanted to know what customers thought and there was no better way to find out than to get feedback from unbiased strangers.

He put each perfume sample through the same research process. Pretending to work for someone else, Ness would approach random strangers on the street and ask for their feedback. "I would say I was from a new fragrance company on the market. I have a survey and would like to know what you think—should we take it to market? I wouldn't tell them I was behind it, because I wanted to get the truth."

Back in the apartment, he tabulated all the responses— five thought it was too sweet, twenty thought it was too strong, etcetera—and then he sent off decisions on how to adjust the formula to the perfumer. What was most surprising was that the comments often matched Ness's own thoughts.

The perfume was now close to perfect, but at the last minute Ness felt the scent needed to be just a little cleaner and requested hints of lavender and watermelon be added to the formula. When the new sample was tested, it received a whopping 95 percent approval rating—an unusually high rating for any perfume. After four long years in development, it was finally perfect. The fragrance—a combination of lavender, watermelon, wildflowers, and herbs—was now ready for the production phase. There was only one stumbling block. Money! All through the development process, Ness had continued to work in B movies, as a seat filler, and as a fragrance model for different companies, but this only created enough income to cover his living expenses.

Help arrived in the form of a friend visiting from New York.

"I told him I had a fragrance, but didn't have any money. I didn't ask him for any, but he said, 'We are going to make this happen. You can pay me back tomorrow or in twenty years.' Then he gave me seventeen thousand dollars. I also maxed out my credit card. I ended up with just enough money to produce one thousand bottles."

Stock bottles and packaging were ordered to keep the costs down and to focus on the quality of the ingredients. Ness was very close to his mother, Laila, who always supported and encouraged his dreams. As a surprise, he not only decided to name the fragrance after her, he secretly copied her signature and silk-screened it on each bottle. Then reality set in. There were one thousand bottles of stock sitting in his apartment, all the money was spent, and no one would buy it. Stores wouldn't even return his calls. He and his roommate had to sell their clothes to make rent and he continued to work as a fragrance model for other companies.

Ness knew there was a market for this perfume. He kept looking for new doors to open and continued to knock on those that were supposedly closed. The Nordstrom buyer where he worked as a fragrance model kindly agreed to give him two minutes of her time, but the news was not good. She told him, "I love your fragrance—it's fantastic— but you have no name and no advertising money. This is harder than show business. I'm just being very honest. There is no way I can do anything with it."

Never one to take no for an answer, he suggested she let him try it in the store and see what happened. Although this had never been tried before, she eventually relented after much persuasion. One hundred bottles were ordered and a time limit of three months established. All unsold product would have to be taken back. It was a small opportunity, but the only one he needed.

Launch day was set for the day before Mother's Day 1995. There was very little time and no money, but that didn't stop Ness from creating an event that would launch him into a brave new world. First, he called in favours from other acting friends. One had a camera and agreed to come, but neither had money to purchase film. Remember, this was the pre-digital era. What he could do was be there and pretend to take photos. After all, who would know there wasn't any film in the camera? All they would see is a photographer snapping images. Others agreed to act as fans to create a buzz of chatter at the opening. The plans were sure to attract the attention of shoppers. A garage sale yielded up a red carpet and a decent suit for the whopping price of five dollars. All the pieces were in place. It was time for the curtain to rise.

When Nordstrom opened its doors, the first thing shoppers saw in the corner was a red carpet. At the end, Ness stood dressed in a suit with bottles of perfume arranged behind him and one of his acting headshots as a backdrop. A flash photographer was busily snapping away. His classmates were talking loudly and offering up comments like, "I can't believe he's here." People quickly began to come over and Ness was ready to work his magic.

"This is Los Angeles; everyone wants to see a star. Before I knew it, I had a line of people coming up and buying. There was one woman in line I will never forget. She had all these diamonds and said to me, 'Darling, I love that suit. It must be from Europe.' I sold out in one hour and had people on the waiting list. I remember walking out the door and there was this homeless person sitting holding his hat. He asked if I had some change. I looked in his hat and said, 'You have more money than I do.'"

So what came next? First, he happily took off his itchy suit. There hadn't been any money to dry clean it and it turned out to have a few resident bugs. Then he jumped in his car to go work as a seat filler for twenty dollars. When they offered him as extra five dollars to be in costume, he happily dressed up as a bag lady feeling grateful for the few extra dollars. Sales in store didn't mean cash in hand. After such a successful launch, Nordstrom was quick to place an order. Right from the start, Ness made it his trademark to build a close relationship with his customers and often dropped into stores for personal appearances. People loved it. Little by little his sales increased, but it was a full three years before he earned enough through perfume sales alone to pay his rent—seven years after he had first started down this road.

During this time, Ness met a producer from the Grammy Awards. The producer's girlfriend loved the scent, so Laila Parfum was asked to participate in their next event. Instead of gift bags, Ness chose to do small samples for the eighteen stars, including Madonna, who were performing that night. The day before, the show publicly mentioned his name in a thank-you. This was great publicity for the new fragrance and the budding celebrity suddenly found himself being invited to more and more insider Hollywood parties. His star was on the rise, but it was a contract with Disney World that took everything to the next level.

Ness had approached Disney World in Florida several times with no response, so in 1998, he decided it was time for a face-to-face meeting with a real person. Norway has its own pavilion in Epcot Theme Park—a part of Disney World. He arranged a meeting first with the store manager and, after showing him a sample, with the buyer. Their initial response was not positive.

"They said, 'Norway is not known for fragrances, so we don't think so.'"

It took a bit of convincing to open the door of opportunity just a crack, but an opportunity was all he needed. The pavilion finally agreed to give the fragrance a try and placed an order. Ness was also asked to come and appear personally. Taking a page from the original Nordstrom launch, he again turned it into a personal event. Laila Parfum was a hit and sold out in five hours. To this day, Disney World is still one of his favourite places to visit.

"I'm there almost every month or two now. It really is the happiest place on earth."

Knowing you have a product you believe in one hundred percent and choosing to be at the front line of sales sharing this passion with customers is a powerful tool. Ness wouldn't have it any other way. Over time his customers have also become his family. They book holidays around his personal appearances and share stories from their lives—both their joys and their sorrows. Two stories quickly come to mind. One is about a couple who met in a bank. She was standing behind her future husband when he noticed this wonderful scent. Turning around, there she was wearing Laila Parfum and the rest is history. The couple even named their daughter Laila. Another story particularly touched his heart.

"I met this woman the other day who told me her daughter who had cancer loved my scent. Her last Christmas, the one present she wanted was a new bottle of my fragrance."

Keeping this personal connection with customers takes a lot of time and energy. Over 85 percent of his time is spent on the road each year leaving very little downtime at home. Getting through airport security, living in hotels, eating in restaurants, and having a serious lack of free time can take its toll, but Ness loves his life and doesn't intend to change any time soon. Every day includes working out. Keeping in the best shape he can helps him deal with the demands created by an intense daily schedule. A positive attitude is also important. There is no room for the words "no, can't" and "shouldn't." He has proved over the years that his take on how to succeed works.

"My fragrance is a very personal thing to me. When I meet people and they meet me, when we tell each other our stories, I get a customer for life. I like when I see them all lit up and happy to see me. I feel blessed. How can I not do this?"

Laila Parfum was launched in 1995. After five years, it brought in a stable income; after six to seven it was a clear success story. In addition to selling in Nordstrom and Disney World, the fragrance now sells in a wide range of boutiques throughout the United States, on thirty-five cruise ships, and in one hundred and fifty locations across Norway, including all the big stores in Oslo. It has been included in gift baskets for numerous high profile events, including the Tony Awards, Grammy Awards, MTV Awards, Miss Universe, Miss Sport Football, and the Eurovision Song Contest.

As Ness firmly believes Laila Parfum is the best fragrance on the market, he decided there would never be another—but there was room for complementary products. First he added a men's scent.

"People kept asking what I was wearing and I realized I needed to come up with something for men. I started with the clean base I used for Laila and then added the natural oils of roots and woods to give it more earth tones. I tested it the same way. It was easy this time, because I asked clients to smell me and give their feedback. Most of the time, women buy the fragrances for their husbands, so it was a great way to connect."

Since its humble beginnings, the brand has grown to include Laila body wash; hand and body cream; body bronzer; lip gloss/plumper; deodorant; scented candles; and purse sets. A new unscented line called "Skin of Norway"—which includes a cleanser, moisturizer, eye gel, mask, and face mist—created from all-natural products—launched in the spring of 2014. It is available only at Epcot Centre in Florida and online at www.laila.com.

Although Ness had succeeded in establishing his brand commercially, he still had another important life goal to meet—that of making a difference in the lives of others. Cancer was one charity that took top priority as his mother and a close friend had waged this difficult battle. With so many female clients, he heard countless stories of their struggles, with breast cancer in particular. In response, he released a special pink bottle with 10 percent of all sales donated to this cause.

Then there was Grete Waitz—a friend from Norway battling ovarian cancer. To assist in fundraising for Waitz's organization—Aktiv mot kreft—Ness joined her New York City Marathon team in 2009. The story of one of his fellow runners inspired Ness—the woman had been shot by her husband, lost an arm, and walked with a limp. She was determined to run anyway. Her story challenged Ness to make his best effort.

"When she was telling me about what had happened to her, I was really impressed. She had such a wonderful energy about her. I decided if she was going to do it, I was going to do it. After eighteen miles, I wanted to give up, but I kept thinking of her the whole time."

He finished the race in four hours and twenty-eight minutes, and raised close to $300,000.

The list of charities Ness contributes time and money to have grown over the years to include Active Against Cancer Foundation, the Los Angeles AIDS Ride, Norwegian Cancer Society, Children's Medical Research Foundation, Susan G. Komen Foundation, Sumo Kids Foundation, Harlem Dowling West Side Centre, The Little Angels Children's Centre, and I Am 4 Kids Foundation, which "teaches kids to decide for themselves who they are and how to become their own role models."

As Ness's customer base is largely women, speaking at various women's groups has become another priority. Motivational talks to disadvantaged children who have nothing also take precedence. When talking to these kids, Ness first has to break down their preconceptions of who he is.

"The kids look at this white guy coming in and think I'm from money. So I begin by telling my story—how I started from nothing. I tell them to think big. That if they really believe and go for it, they can make it happen."

Letters From a Son to His Mother was released in 2009. Dedicated to his mother, Ness penned the pocket book to show her his love and appreciation, and to share an even wider message—everyone needs love and support to become all they can be. To this day, his mother is still his staunchest supporter, offering words that guide him daily such as, "Never give up on your dreams" and "With hard work and dedication you will succeed." With many years of experience behind him, Ness is following in her footsteps by offering words of wisdom to others, all gleaned from his years of building the Laila brand. They are laid out in his press kit under the title Business Model.

- Coming from a humble and hardworking family in Norway, my road to success here in the States was a long and rocky one. While things were difficult, I kept practising the advice I received from my mother when I was a younger teenager—and I still live by today!
- To be successful in life you have to believe in yourself first, before you even consider stepping into the business world. Every dream can come true! You can do anything you wish and be successful as long as you have faith and believe in your dreams.
- Always keep your goals in sight and never accept "no" as "the final answer." Be passionate about your business

and understand it is not only about money, but long-term success. There will always be doors closing, but it is up to you to open up the next one. Never stop working on your skills and expertise. Never stop learning. Each day gives you new opportunities. And don't be afraid of asking for help—it deprives others of the pleasure of helping you grow.

- An excellent entrepreneur never forgets the hard days and remembers to be thankful to the people who helped him to become who he is today.

In 2013, Ness launched a new campaign—"HANDling With Care." The plan is to travel to every major city in the United States, booking personal appearances, speaking engagements, and trunk shows. In each, he will set aside one afternoon to visit a centre for individuals dealing with serious physical and/or mental challenges. Therapeutic touch—hence the all-caps "HAND"—has made headlines for its ability to help patients heal, ease pain, improve quality of life, and even shorten recovery time. As a trained masseur, Ness will give back by giving of himself—providing patients with personal, one-on-one hand massages.

Geir Ness's path to success was fuelled not only by his mother's support, unflinching optimism, and sheer hard work, but also by the compassion he feels for those around him. It has never been just about creating financial success or about giving money to charities. Ness offers himself personally to the people he meets in all areas of his work. These two aspects of his life—business and charity—cannot be separated as they walk hand in hand.

Patricia Fieldwalker

"I like to be told I'm childish. I think it's a wonderful thing to be. I think it's a terrible thing to have none of the child left in you."

The history of women's lingerie goes back centuries. In fact, its first historical reference is from Egypt in 3000 B.C. Lingerie was the ultimate sign of luxury reserved for the upper class. Each culture that embraced lingerie changed how they expressed it. Each time a new era redefined what beauty meant, its expression again altered.

Over the years, these scandalous undergarments flattened, conformed, moulded, assisted with hygiene, enticed, and preserved modesty. While we sometimes raise our eyebrows at the vintage shape-altering laced corsets and hoop skirts of previous decades, the practice of altering our figure still exists today in the form of push-up bras and numerous other types of body shapers.

Our modern concept of lingerie began to evolve some time near the end of the 18th century and took serious hold in the early 1900s. Corsets were no longer mandatory as more comfortable brassieres took their place. Lingerie became sexier. There were still smaller shape-altering trends that encouraged women into uncomfortable girdles (1920s to 1960s) or pointy bras (1950s to today). But the trend has slowly and consistently moved toward beauty and comfort.

Lingerie found a new expression when it began to be exposed openly. Bras, chemises, and even gowns were incorporated into the wardrobe as day and evening wear. The only negative trend to emerge was that of mass production. Suddenly the stores were filled with piles of uncomfortable polyester and scratchy lace. The price was low, but the wearing experiences unpleasant. Fortunately, there are still designers offering women truly inspired and luxurious options. One such designer is Patricia Fieldwalker—an industry icon.

It's been a long time since Fieldwalker sat down at a sewing machine and created that first silk camisole to wear on a date with her husband. That one moment was the starting point of an amazing journey. She ended up owning a successful luxury lingerie brand, experienced an exciting trip to Paris where her collection triumphantly rocked the runways, and then had to suffer through the ultimate low of losing everything in 1992 because of outside investors. Life then brought her back full circle, returning the designer to her roots to rebuild the company from scratch as sole owner. Losing everything was a hard lesson. Today, the designer enjoys the intimacy and full control of having no one to answer to, and her beautifully crafted luxury lingerie is recognized and sold all over the world.

Despite many challenges faced along the way and a changing market intent on mass production, the brand's focus has never wavered. Each collection features exquisite colours, buttery silks, soft French lace, and couture tailoring that includes difficult bias cuts and intricate tuxedo tucks. Cheaply made knock-offs abound, but truth be told, the designer has no interest in creating anything less than top quality garments. Nothing goes out the door unless it is one hundred percent perfect by her high standards, from construction right down to having the thread colour be an exact match. These garments are beautiful works of art, investment pieces meant to be intrinsic parts of a woman's wardrobe for years to come.

"The fabric is incredibly expensive; the lace is imported from France. I can't afford anyone making a mistake. I am a real dictator when it comes to the designs, including the colour of the thread. If I'm going to put my name on it, I'm embarrassed if it's not really good."

Fieldwalker didn't originally plan on a career in the fashion industry; it was fate in its best form—a decision, that led to a path, that took her to a career she loves. The designer has never had any formal training—impressive given the fact her garments are known for their incredible fit and couture construction. The credit goes to her mother and aunts.

"My mother and her sisters were all talented dressmakers, so my mum sewed for us all the time. We were never taught to sew—we wanted her to do it—but somehow learned by default. As kids we were always the best dressed. One year she took us to a local fair—the Pacific National Exhibition—dressed in, of all things, little black-and-brown herringbone coats with velvet collars. Come on!"

Her mother embraced a very elegant, low-key European style that included wonderful fabrics, beautiful colours, and classic silhouettes—an aesthetic she passed on to her daughter.

These early influences would have to be put on hold for a while, as Fieldwalker's father was the opposite. He loved science. Fieldwalker had no choice but to attend university and enter this area of study. She begrudgingly applied to the University of British Columbia and, once accepted, began to make the best of the situation. Unfortunately for her father, only a short time passed before reality set in.

"I despised science—slide rules, mathematics, chemistry, etcetera. After one year that was the end of that. I asked myself what I could do that I was interested in, and it was English, of course. Then I started getting interested in sociology, especially the subfield of deviance. My professor in deviance used to have a night job as a taxi driver, just to get to talk with people. These things were a lot more interesting than working with a slide rule."

While deviance was an exciting area of studies to explore, the field wouldn't have been a good career to embrace as Fieldwalker fully admits to being way too empathetic. Whether people are in crisis or animals are in need—their burden is her burden. Charity work in many forms has provided an outlet for that empathetic side, a way to make a difference for those in need. One example is Fieldwalker's concern for stray dogs. To this day she buys toys for the SPCA.

"One day I read those poor animals are depressed, because they are abandoned and they need stuff to play with. So I thought, 'I can do that.' Once a month I collect toys and things to donate."

What she cannot do is see the dogs that will get the toys. Why? It is too hard for her to see them in cages.

After graduating from university, Fieldwalker's first job was as the Assistant Director for a local community centre, responsible for registering people in programs. A man passed her while she was driving to work one day in her little blue MG Midget; he happened to catch a glimpse, and was instantly taken. He immediately turned around and followed her to work. From the moment she laid eyes on him, it was clearly destiny at work.

"It's a very romantic story. Rol walked into the centre, came up to my desk, and registered for a Silk Screening class. I was actually engaged to someone else at the time, but told the course instructor I'd just signed up the most handsome man I'd ever laid eyes on for her class. After a few classes, he came to ask if he could purchase some ink from me. Despite the fact I was wearing a ring, when I took him to the storeroom, he asked if I'd consider having dinner with him one night. I replied, 'I'd be delighted.'"

Off came the ring and only nine months later, they were married.

Next a position opened up to work as Associate Director of the International House at the University of British Columbia. It lasted for three wonderful years.

"Students from all over the world came here. Each had their own organizations and a lot of them were very political. There were many heated debates between those students and me. It was an intense but very interesting time, and I met a lot of fantastic people."

Then one day, the designer decided she had been married long enough; it was time to have kids. Always one who knew her mind and trusted her instincts, she quit her job.

Fieldwalker fully admits this wasn't a decision made logically. It was an intuitive choice made while dealing with other considerations. She and her husband were only renting a little house and money wasn't plentiful, but when the owners decided to sell, the couple made the decision to take on a mortgage. Then their first child arrived and eighteen months later, a set of twins. This time still holds fond memories for Fieldwalker, despite the inevitable chaos.

"They were like three little birds. I would line them up in their high chairs and go bam, bam, bam. Of course, I had to nurse the twins, because I had nursed 'the prince' and there was no way, just because there were two of them, they wouldn't get the same thing. My husband called me the dairy queen."

All three were boys—all little tigers—each wanting attention.

The designer has somehow married the two sides of her nature into a unique, unified whole. One side is her love of producing something exquisitely perfect; every detail must be right. The other is a true sense of childlike magic. Working in her company's design studio creating beautiful garments offered an outlet for the first. Family was a place where the second—her love of magic—could be expressed and there was no time where this became more apparent than at Christmas time.

"I've always adored Christmas. I started the boys sleeping

under the Christmas tree as soon as they were out of cribs. My husband says I'm crazy, but I have this thing about magic. I believe in it. My mantra is 'romance, adventure, and magic.' I always read my kids fairy tales and my eldest in particular loved them. When we were reading *The Lord of the Rings*, he was so into it, I went out and bought him a bag of runes. He tried to learn to write with them."

Fate entered quietly into the midst of all this mayhem. Fieldwalker and her husband were to attend a play. The future designer had an idea way ahead of its time to pair a quality silk and lace camisole with her suit—an innate knack that has kept her well ahead of the trends all through her career. While a common look now—back in the late 1970s her husband found the idea of showing one's underwear scandalous. The camisole and suit combination did win out, but it took a bit of doing. There wasn't a quality silk and French lace camisole to be found anywhere in Vancouver.

"It was all polyester and synthetic blends; nothing good. I thought, 'I can do this. It's quite simple.' So I made myself a camisole and wore it to the play. My husband was embarrassed as he is very reserved, but I felt you could hardly see it."

In fact, he spent much of the night trying to cover her up. While her husband might not have been a fan, many friends were quite taken with the look. First, one asked if she could have a camisole made, then another, then a husband ordered one as a gift for his wife's birthday. Week by week, the business just kept growing and she slowly added a few new items to the line. All the while, Fieldwalker was embroiled in the daily life of three small but active dynamos who demanded attention.

"I had nothing to do—RIGHT?"

Soon the house was overrun with the trappings of a production studio—silk fabric, thread, lace, and more. Her husband finally stepped in and rented a small space for her to work in. One seamstress was now on staff to help meet production demands.

Next, an enthusiastic mentor decided to help Fieldwalker by setting up a meeting with buyers from a former department store chain called Eaton's. The only problem was the designer really didn't understand what was expected.

"In came the Eaton's buyers. My cutting table was covered and stuff was everywhere. There were a just few garments hanging. The buyers were waiting for me to show them my line and I didn't even know what that meant. I said, 'Here's this one and then there's that one.' By this time I was getting kind of excited, so I was crawling under the table to pull out more fabric. 'I've got this great piece and we could do blah, blah, blah.' It was probably the least professional presentation they had ever seen and by the time they left the room, I had no idea what had happened."

Even though the presentation wasn't polished and her collection only consisted of four pieces—camisole, half-slip, chemise, and cover up—the company buyers called two weeks later to place an order for the holiday season. It was the biggest to date. Exciting? Yes! BUT ... there really wasn't enough time to finish everything without more help.

She brought in a second seamstress and the three of them worked late into the wee hours, sometimes not stopping until they were seeing spots. A third seamstress was found. On delivery day, the boxes of garments were dropped off in person to the warehouse. It was the beginning of what would become a phenomenal period of growth.

A second local store soon picked up the line. Then out of the blue, Fieldwalker was approached by an experienced salesman who wanted to represent the brand. As soon as a contract was in place, he was off to Seattle with his sights set on the high-end Nordstrom chain. The quality of the lingerie—something not seen in North America at the time—impressed the store's buyers, and he returned to Vancouver with an order in hand.

The increased demand on production meant a larger workspace was needed, so she found a new location. Having cracked the US market, the sales rep was now eager to head to New York City. The trip ultimately brought in a new client who sealed the brand's name as true luxury goods.

As an experienced salesman, Fieldwalker's rep realized he had the right product at the right time. This was the era of the television show *Dynasty*, where luxury was the order of the day. Nothing was too over the top. He had in hand a top quality, couture line of lingerie and there was only limited competition. Most of what was available was awful—made out of uncomfortable synthetics and scratchy domestic lace. There were challenges—such as a lack of money to finance a trip—but the salesman was determined. If the company could put up the airfare, he would sleep in the airport. Wisely the answer was yes.

Fieldwalker remembers this time like it was yesterday.

"His first appointment was with Lord and Taylor, and we knew there would be a number of vendors showing their lines at the same time. Each was assigned a change room, and the buyer—a woman—came by with a little cane, flicked the curtain open, and after glancing for only a second and half went, 'Um. Not today.' That was the end."

Fortunately, his second appointment at Bergdorf Goodman was more successful. The store loved the collection and ended up spending three hours with the rep. Their order also meant success for the Patricia Fieldwalker label.

"It's like the blessing of the Virgin Mary. If Bergdorf Goodman takes you, that's it. Everybody who is serious shops there. If they see you there, they don't wonder if the quality is okay, if it really fits you, or if it ships on time."

It is a relationship that proved to be a lifeline in an upcoming crisis.

Next came a whirlwind of notoriety and rapid growth. Magazine spreads, outside investors, and the runways in Paris followed in quick order. Fieldwalker was photographed along with her models standing in front of Bergdorf Goodman—the iconic New York shopping destination. The first big lingerie show in Paris was definitely one of the early high points, which still brings back fond memories.

"Again, it was the right place at the right time. Back then, the lingerie runway shows were very French with models coming out holding umbrellas. We came in like North American gangbusters and people went nuts."

Instead of the traditional Parisian music, speakers pounded the booming beats of American tunes. There was a show every hour pulling in huge crowds. While her collection did include softer looks, the designer chose to showcase powerful colours such as tangerine, green, and purple—eye-popping in the sea of traditional white, pink, and pastels shown by other labels. The experience was amazing.

Success on the runway in Paris brought in an international clientele. New markets opened up in Europe, Japan, Saudi Arabia, and further afield. The business grew very quickly and the company was taken public, a decision Fieldwalker would later come to regret. The designer now owned a state-of-the-art production studio full of first-rate equipment. On staff were two to three pattern drafters, two to three sample makers, and sixty seamstresses. Any new design idea could move quickly from first conception to reality.

Fieldwalker continued to show her collection on the runway in Paris from 1984 to 2005 and was winner of "le Ruban de Madame Figaro" award at the Salon International de la Lingerie for best in show in 1988. It was an inspiring time that revolved around designing, going to shows, and buying luxury fabrics and lace, but in the background, a storm was brewing. English banks were having a lot of problems in Europe with outstanding debts and had decided to divest some of their Canadian portfolio. Her company was one of those put on the chopping block.

"We moved way too fast and didn't have enough control of the company's growth. There was a lot of excitement about the fact we were selling, but not enough focus was put on collecting money owed. Some of our European accounts were ninety days overdue."

A European satellite office was in the works that would have given them someone local who spoke the language to handle these accounts, but it came too late. With only one week's notice, the company was plunged into receivership.

This dealt Fieldwalker a devastating blow. This company was her baby, built from the ground up. She couldn't eat, couldn't sleep—she was terrified. Buyers were circling and everyone wanted a piece. Top equipment, fabulous fabrics and laces, exclusive patterns, and more were all up for grabs. They knew the line was a phenomenal success and enjoyed a first-class reputation. Everyone wanted to cash in. The most devastating loss was her patterns. The sale left her with nothing—not even the use of her label.

"What was so horrible was that these people were going to make deals using the fabric under the counters to make anything they wanted. I said, 'Wait a minute. You can't put my name on anything I haven't designed.' The guy replied, 'Patricia, I can put your name on a baseball cap if I want.' So it wasn't nice."

After it was all over, Fieldwalker was a wreck, but not defeated. She found strong support from many industry friends, including long-time customer Bergdorf Goodman.

At the time, this company worked like a family and all the merchants were referred to as friends of the store. Their buyer called to offer support, and reassured the designer she didn't need to make a trip to New York. They loved her line and just wanted her to make whatever she could for Christmas—even if it was only a little bit. "Just put it in a box and send it."

The next guardian angel was a friend—Neil Tissington— who owned a building with an empty floor and some old machines she could use. These were the very same machines she had started out on. Shoulders back and head held high, she began to rebuild. The new company was called Adagio, "because the adagio dance in ballet is so beautiful and it's a dance for two people." This later became "Adagio by Patricia Fieldwalker," then "Patricia Fieldwalker for Adagio" and finally what it is today—the "Patricia Fieldwalker Adagio Collection."

Through all the ups and downs, there was one partner she still embraced fully—her husband Rol. An architect by trade and artist at heart, he has the same love of creating beauty, the same perfectionist nature, the same humanitarian spirit.

"Rol is a man for all seasons: intelligent, passionate about the world we live in, committed to Architecture with a big A and its role in nurturing the human spirit. He's honest, kind, and still a gorgeous man. Perhaps the lady doth protest too much, but it's all true!"

They are on the same page. He is president and co-owner, signs the cheques, and works with the bookkeeper to look after the business end. There are times her husband does try to influence the production end, but with only very limited success.

"He tells me all the time that the line is too big and I keep trying to scale it down." The truth is, even if she drops one look, she has so many other ideas in the works that a new one steps in pretty quickly to take its place. And designs are hard to let go of as she loves them all.

From the ashes, Fieldwalker has rebuilt her business to what it is today. It is still known the world over for first-class luxury garments created from the highest quality fabrics and trimmed with beautiful French lace. The client list still includes accounts in Canada, the United States, and Europe. Bergdorf Goodman offers her lingerie in a special in-store boutique. Two collections are offered per year, with small additions created for Valentine's Day, Christmas, etcetera. Fieldwalker is content to stay out of the marketing whirlwind with its inherent risks and embrace the success that comes from offering a quality product and a well-tuned finger on the pulse of where trends are heading.

"Here I am. It's much smaller, but I will never have partners again. If I'm going down, it's because I made the mistake and I know what's going on. In a way, it's much nicer now, because I don't have to answer to anyone. I don't have a bank on my back wanting a report every seven seconds. And I still have the same few sewers I've had since starting over."

Things did have to change. The company is now a custom

design house that does not carry stock. With few exceptions, customers have to pay a 50 percent deposit when they place an order and absolutely no work is started until the deposit has been received. The balance must be paid in full before the order ships.

"We are like a little atelier. You tell us what you want from the samples we show you, we get the fabric, we dye the lace, and we make it for you. No one can afford to be somebody else's banker, especially now."

Another change was to skip the big runway shows and booths in large trade shows. The collection would now be shown to buyers in a private hotel suite through one-on-one appointments. The new business direction proved to be just the right formula as the Patricia Fieldwalker Adagio Collection grew steadily over the next few years.

In 2011, an enormous earthquake of 9.0 magnitude rocked Japan. Centred off the Pacific Coast of Tōhoku, it was the most powerful ever recorded in Japan's history and left hundreds of people dead, injured, or missing. A deadly tsunami followed, sweeping inland, swamping towns, washing away a train, and igniting massive fires. The devastation was unimaginable and the pictures were heart-breaking. A cry for aid came from many organizations and those with family living in the country were overcome with worry. Those watching in North America scrambled to answer the call.

The designer's heart instantly went out to all the people struggling and trying to deal with the destruction. She also had a personal connection that made this suffering all too real. Her nephew was married to a woman from Japan. This woman's entire family was still living there and worry for their welfare deeply affected her extended Canadian family.

One day Fieldwalker and her husband stopped by their favourite local Japanese restaurant for a bite. The owner was running an earthquake benefit by offering a particular special and donating most of the money. Of course, they ordered the special. It felt good, but she wanted to do more. Giving back had been an important part of her business from day one and this cause drew her. The only question was, how best to make a difference?

Vancouver Fashion Week (VFW) was coming up short-ly and Fieldwalker was already scheduled to show her collection. That meant exposure to lots of people both at the opening gala and on the day of her show. Creative by nature, the ideas flowed. The first to catch fire was origami cranes. Legend has it that anyone who folds a thousand origami cranes will be granted a wish—a perfect idea to inspire. A group of the designer's friends were quickly as-sembled to help fold all the miniature cranes. These origa-mi birds would be used to solicit donations. Some were left in a bowl at the Japanese restaurant to inspire customers to give. Fieldwalker would take the rest to VFW to encourage donations from those attending. The suggested minimum donation was ten dollars.

Kimonos were already an important part of her current collection, so the designer used that as a launching point.

"I bought beautiful heart boxes. My daughter-in-law—a

wonderful graphic designer—also created a beautiful heart design for the cover. I said, 'We now need an open heart— open your heart to Japan.' At the opening gala and at the end of our runway show, I put the girls in the kimonos and they circulated through the crowd holding the beautiful heart boxes with slots taking donations. I can't remember how much money we raised, but I was disappointed as I wanted to raise millions!"

Everything was given to the restaurant as they had the local connections in Japan to make sure the money made a real difference.

As soon as this fundraiser was over, others took its place, as giving back has always been, and always will be, a part of her focus. The reason? To make a tangible difference in the lives of others. Fieldwalker gives on a regular basis to A Loving Spoonful—a Greater Vancouver volunteer-driven charity that provides free, nutritious meals to people living with HIV/AIDS. She raises money to educate girls in China, and more. Wherever she can find a way to be of service she steps in.

"I guess in some way, what I do contributes to how a woman feels about herself, but not seriously enough to say that's the key point of her life. I would take more pride in saying I was a doctor without borders really doing something of serious value."

Every day, when Fieldwalker walks into her studio, there is a sense of aaahhh. So many things here create a feeling of joy. First there is the small staff of seamstresses who have worked with her for many years and who have become like family. Then comes colour, which probably inspires her design work the most. The current season's beautiful palette catches her eye each morning and—whether single colours for the palette, unique combinations in a single garment, or creating beautiful one-of-a-kind prints—it is where she truly has the Midas touch.

"Colour is absolutely important and I think I have a really good eye for it. I see a lot of collections and think, 'That's a really cute piece, but the colour … ' For me, it needs to be a little bit of cosmetic—[enhancing a client's natural beauty]—so you can't go too crazy. My job is also to design, not copy. If everybody is going to come out with purple, I don't want purple. I want something else."

Last there are luxurious fabrics she loves—an appreciation handed down from her mother. The silks are like butter, the laces ultrasoft and elegant.

Running your own business is always stressful. There are challenges with customers, supplies, shipping, deadlines, staff who are ill or on vacation, seven-day workweeks during rush times, and slim profit margins. Then there is the changing market that is obsessed with logoed merchandise (even if poorly made), bulk goods manufactured in Third World countries, and trendy, modern designs that will be here today and gone tomorrow, over well-made classic pieces that can carry a wardrobe for the next decade. Many companies now pressure designers to carry stock so they can order a piece at a time, impossible for a couture atelier.

"Sometimes I feel like I'm selling milk in bottles. It's like trying to force gourmet food on somebody who wants to eat McDonald's. You have to really love what you do because it's not a career, it's a love affair."

Another concern is skilled labour. The climate in North America now pushes students to embrace higher education and the trades are looked down on as only being for those who cannot cut it in school. Production jobs are increasingly being sent overseas where there are very low wages and poor working conditions, instead of creating training programs here. Fieldwalker feels there needs to be a shift to treating jobs of every kind as respectful paths to follow.

"We have given away the jobs. No wonder we have non-working poor. If someone has some level of skill, is honest, dependable, and can do the work, there are no mid-range jobs for them. It's awful."

Pairing the stress of work with a perfectionist nature can mean trouble if it can't be left behind when you return home. Fieldwalker found a truly unique solution—a very large dog. The designer has always loved dogs, but her husband felt with three active boys in the house and both of them in demanding careers, there was no time or energy to embrace a pet. Then things changed. Rol began to get winded when he was out on walks. At the doctor's, he received the mother of all diagnoses. He not only needed a coronary bypass—he needed six! This was a complicated operation and a big part of Rol's recovery was exercise, especially walking. With the nest now empty, he decided it was the right time to bring a dog into their lives. She was over the moon.

Fieldwalker wisely decided to step back and leave the decision to Rol. The story of his two-year journey to finding just the right new family member still brings a smile to her face. First, he researched the history of dogs and each breed's qualities. The final decision—a Rhodesian Ridgeback—a phenomenal animal originally bred in South Africa, used as both hunting dogs and to protect the family. Then her husband spent an entire month visiting a breeder every Saturday to just sit with the puppies. He created a diagram of what made for the perfect proportions—shoulder height, ideal weight, musculature, stance, movement, coat colour, and overall appearance—which he presented to the breeder. In the end, how could the breeder say no to such a determined and well-informed adoptive parent?

Beau Bijoux's En Avant Gryphon—"Gryph" or "Cuddle Bunny" to his friends—is a 110-pound mountain of joy who has become an intricate part of their daily lives. Fieldwalker is totally smitten and Gryph has proven the perfect distraction from the stress of work.

"This is the dog to beat all dogs. In the mornings, I wake up and think I don't want to go to work and deal with the usual complications in production. Then he comes over with a wet nose and starts kissing my face. By the time I get out of bed, he's dancing around and happy to see me. I get home feeling beat, then see my dog and ask if he wants to go for a walk. He gets all nuts."

Gryph also creates the most laundry as he loves to be clean as a cat, right down to his bedding. To keep him warm at night, Fieldwalker donated her old Ralph Lauren cashmere sweater to keep him warm. Eventually the neck of the sweater became too tight, so Gryph now sports a pair of fleece pyjamas purchased from an online store. Problem solved!

In 2014, Fieldwalker received two emails that made her heart sing. The first came from friend and corset designer Melanie Talkington to let her know one of Fieldwalker's teddies—a stunning silk, black lace charmeuse creation circa 1985—was on display in New York City in the Museum of FIT's (Fashion Institute of Technology's) exhibition titled "Exposed: A History of Lingerie." This curated show traced developments in intimate apparel from the 18th century to the present. It was an amazing honour and an affirmation of all that her brand stands for. Buying a beautiful, quality garment is an investment that will grace your closet for years.

The second email came from Sheena Ward, editor of a celebrity fan blog called Haus of Rihanna. The well-known celebrity had been seen on the street sporting a stunning deep pink, spaghetti strap, silk gown paired with a denim jacket. Was it one of Fieldwalker's? Yes. The designer couldn't hold back her excitement.

"I am on a roll! My gown on a millennium glamour girl ... who says classics can't be groovy?"

The sighting also confirmed what the designer had always known in her heart—classics do not go out of style, they just find a new expression.

As the market continues to shift, Fieldwalker has looked

to new marketing opportunities such as e-tail spaces that will let her reach out to the growing, very affluent generation of boomer women who shop daily online. What will not change is her commitment to producing luxurious, well-made, classic lingerie she can be proud of.

"I'm not interested in working in less expensive fabrics or lace. There are a million people out there doing that right now—even people who used to be high quality. Mine is a custom house where people are investing money in things they expect to last a really long time. We don't do novelty. The boomer market is there. These are confident women who don't need to dress up like a show girl or a dominatrix to feel sensuous. These are classic beauties who have a sense of elegance—think Grace Kelly, Audrey Hepburn, and now Julianna Margulies, Cate Blanchett, and Nicole Kidman."

With so many years in the business, how does Fieldwalker define success? Her answer has nothing to do with money or career.

"Happy family, good kids, being a good mum—that's more important to me than anything. That and standing your ground. The kids have always been allowed to have an opinion. Then we would argue and fight, and then it was over. But we still love each other. It's a life lesson for them."

Whatever the next few years hold and wherever her journey takes her, you can be sure she will keep family front and centre, and her love of colour and beautifully made things will always find an expression.

Pamela Masik

"Art is a life-long journey—you never stop learning. Every time you pick up the paintbrush or a piece of clay, it's like life, and going into that humbly is a really good place. "Someone once said to me, 'You're talented.' I said, 'I work hard.'"

In every civilization throughout history, you will find culture, spirituality, sorrow, and joy expressed through fine art. When words are not enough, art steps in to communicate for us in a way that defies language barriers. It is a broad field that encompasses performance, design, mixed media, prints, sculpture, and photography, but probably we are most connected with painting. Everywhere we turn, we find canvases that range from beautiful to distorted, from classic to avant-garde, and from lighter subject matter to those with deep and sometimes disturbing meanings. Many of us love to dabble in our spare time, but for serious artists, art is a passion that wells up from deep within. For Pamela Masik, it is her life.

Art is an obsession for Masik. It is a call that must be answered. Ideas flow like a mighty river and she responds in kind—working on more than twenty canvases and sculptures at the same time. When inspiration for a new series arrives, it is never accompanied by a thought of what will sell commercially. The goal is to convey a message. *The Forgotten, Requiem, Engagement, The Caged Bird, Revelation,* and *Corkscrew Follies*—titles of some of her collections—all challenge us to look at their messaging on a deeply personal level. These collections are each chapters in the story of her dual journey as both an artist and a human being.

Masik grew up in Thunder Bay, Ontario—one of seven children. Life was not easy. Violence and abuse were a staple right from the beginning and finding a way to cope was important. As with most people who come from this kind of upbringing, she prefers not to discuss it. That doesn't mean these experiences are hidden away. Art is where she shares openly and freely about every aspect of life's challenges. The chaos during her childhood led her on an inward journey where—starting at a very young age—she discovered the joy of artistic expression.

"I have this early memory of drawing a picture of my sister looking through a fish tank with all the fish swimming around. I took one of Paul Klee's paintings and mimicked some of his shapes."

Being immersed in creating art through drawing, painting, clay sculpture, and photography offered much needed moments of peace. Everything and everyone were subjects to be explored. As no one at home was particularly interested in her pieces, Masik gave most of her artwork away to school friends.

Team sports was another important diversion. Participating in sports was a welcome respite from the realities of everyday life. Sports offered supportive team-mates, a positive environment, recognition of her talent, and hard physical exercise to reduce her stress. Although it seems a contradiction to be accomplished both as an artist and an athlete, Masik was an exception who excelled at both.

"In the summer of my senior year, I played provincial finals volleyball and the coach at the university in Thunder Bay discussed the opportunity to play for Lakehead University. Was I interested?" As much as she loved playing, her heart answered, "No."

Although quite shy by nature, Masik is an entrepreneur at heart—a talent that many of those with an artistic temperament lack. Early on she learned the value of determination, drive, and goal setting. There wasn't a lot of money in the budget at home, so to participate in sports, she had to come up with the money herself. By age nine she had her first job, and by her teen years was working private commissions, painting billboards for local businesses.

She applied the same skill set used to drum up business to get sponsorship for athletic travels. If there was an upcoming trip, her grandmother would drive her around to local businesses to meet with the company presidents and boldly offer her spiel. "I would get really creative with them saying, 'I can't afford this trip. What I can give you in return for your donation is a tax write-off and a picture of our team.'" This talent would prove invaluable in the future.

Internally, it was a different picture. In emotional turmoil and highly sensitive to others, Masik struggled to be comfortable in social situations.

"I am very much in tune with people on a deep level. When I meet someone it's more like an energy for me. It's a lot to hold on to."

Most of her school years were spent floating between the groups—not tightly connected to one in particular. She also struggled at this time with a serious bout of depression. Back then, no one knew what depression was and just assumed the person was sick. It had to be dealt with privately as best one could. A heavy burden on any teenager's shoulders.

She considered several options after high school—even Marine Biology—but exploring Italy won out. Masik still remembers this life-changing time.

"I was curious. I was a seeker. I was someone who pushed myself and got into a lot of trouble. I was also really innocent in many ways. My high school sweetheart was Italian, so I decided to go to Italy and learn about his culture. Deep down I think that was just the story I told everyone because I needed to get out of Thunder Bay."

With only five hundred dollars in her pocket, she stepped onto the plane full of nervous excitement. This was pre-internet and the world was still a very large and mysterious place.

Masik looked out of the windows as the plane was descending and was stunned by the view of a countryside awash with colours she had never seen before—a blending of lemons, olive trees, and the soft hues of the Mediterranean landscape. Living in Italy was also a revelation. Every day offered new experiences that opened her eyes to other cultures and deepened her growing curiosity about the world.

"I had a fear about going, but it ended up setting me free. Seeing how the locals socialized and dressed, I learned about the art of life. Even the least attractive person was beautiful because of the way they carried themselves—their grace, the scarf around their neck, their little coffees. It was an experience I will never forget."

It was a time of freedom and exploration accompanied by an informal gang of cohorts—going around on what was literally a glorified red bike with an engine, the rest of her friends on upscale Vespa scooters. One night, the group of girls got into trouble while eating in a local restaurant. To this day she has no idea why. Her best guess is that it had something to do with the girl who disappeared into the wine cellar with a young man. Lots of shouting ensued in Italian that she couldn't follow. Then they were kicked out and chased by the police. Knowing her older scooter would not keep up, she chose to take a shortcut home.

"It was getting really dark. I had the bike on full throttle as the last section of the dirt road was up a steep hill. Bats were flying around me. At the last minute, I had to crank the throttle, jump off the bike, and run up the hill or I wouldn't have made it."

Despite the camaraderie, she began to feel very alone. Romance was blooming all around, but it wasn't knocking on her door. It was time to head home.

On return to Canada a year later, Masik entered an unfocused time of her life—a time of looking for a new path. She had some serious down moments. First was a brief stint studying Massage Therapy in Toronto. When that didn't feel right, she was off to a job in a restaurant/bar. There the sex, drugs, and rock-n-roll lifestyle called. A very difficult couple of years came next, fuelled by issues from her difficult childhood.

"When you grow up in an abusive environment, you usually end up abusing yourself. You let people into your life who do the same. I was in a really dark place."

Waking up one morning, she realized there wouldn't be a good ending on this path; she chose to walk away. That meant leaving both job and friends behind. Mexico called.

Masik wanted a clean break from everyday life, so in a spontaneous moment she walked into a travel agency and two days later hopped on a plane by herself. A surprise awaited her, one that would change her life forever—young, fresh, and innocent love. The memories are still strong today.

"It was very romantic, fun and—perhaps in hindsight—naive. But even to this day, the long walks through the old town along cobblestone streets and horseback riding along the beach still live. Even though we were young and naive, that kind of loving without abandon is what any hopeless romantic lives for."

He was from Vancouver; she was still living in Eastern Canada. It was difficult to say goodbye when the time came to return home.

At first the young lovers tried to make it work long-distance, but the miles proved impossible to bear. Masik packed her bags and headed for the West Coast. It wasn't long before she found herself pregnant and nine months later, the mother of a beautiful boy. It is still the highest moment of her life. Although in the end the relationship did not stand the test of time, and those early years as a single mother held many challenges, she wouldn't have it any other way. Her son was and continues to be one of her greatest joys.

"My son is my angel. He made me really look at myself so I could become a better mother and a better person. I had to learn new ways to take care of myself. The one thing in my life that I really want to know I have succeeded at is that I've raised a respectful man."

Throughout this time, the artist was employed by Buschlen Mowatt—a high-end Vancouver gallery featuring internationally recognized artists—where she sold art to monied collectors. Executive dress was the order of the day. She donned the traditional suit. While her days were consumed with work at the gallery, the artist dedicated nights to developing a new internet business and producing her own original paintings. She would offer these in her online gallery anonymously. It was disheartening when they didn't sell.

Masik was exploring the potential of a new technology—the internet. She was one of the first to launch an online art gallery and she was writing a blog long before it became a popular pastime in social media circles. Working capital for the project was provided by student business loans. The artist used cutting-edge programs not yet in common use for her innovative website. Virtual tours of artwork for sale were a reality on her web gallery years before they were ever used in the real estate industry.

Then one day she saw herself in the media dressed in business attire and her world shifted.

"Here I am in a business suit trying to sell the work of other people and none of my own was selling. Then I saw my picture in the newspaper and I think I almost had a nervous breakdown. I saw myself in that business suit—so young, trying to be so serious, trying to be taken seriously—and I realized it wasn't who I was."

Masik decided to strip herself entirely of that persona. Everything went—the car, the clothes, the furniture, the nice apartment. All was pawned, sold, or given away. She moved with her son into a cheap apartment in a rundown part of town. She shaved her head—a significant personal statement. Dinner was often peanut butter and jelly sandwiches, their table just a cardboard box. More than once the pair had to sneak down the fire escape when their rent was late, her wallet empty, and the landlord at the door. Fortunately, he would sometimes agree to collect his rent later when her work sold. As she rolled pennies and tried to figure out how to support herself and her son, everyone just kept telling her to get a job.

Over the next three years, Masik painted feverishly while working on healing her mind, body, and soul. She had acupuncture to deal with back and neck injuries from a serious car accident, attended seminars in personal growth and how to be your authentic self, she read books, studied philosophers, and enjoyed therapy. The journey was about finally letting go of the past and moving forward. It was about learning how to live in the world in a healthy way. She asked lots of questions and in the end found the needed answers.

"All through this stage I was talking to myself—'This is how I see my life. This is what I want to do.'—and I envisioned myself creating these huge paintings. In the end I realized if you have a dream, follow it, and everything else will come."

It was time now to move forward and embrace the future with open arms, but it wasn't easy. Her pockets were empty; the cupboards were bare. Some days it wasn't clear where their next meal would come from. Masik found herself struggling with anger about the years living in a dark place, haunted by her upbringing and her choice to escape into drugs and alcohol to numb the pain. There were moments of feeling unworthy and that nothing she created had any value. She was ashamed. Choosing to put herself out as an artist challenged that negative inner voice, but it was an important step in healing.

"I had to learn self-love. I would stand there with my hand trembling trying to paint—worried that the next brush stroke would mess up the whole thing. I had to overcome that fear."

Masik chose to start by copying the paintings of the Old Masters. Then she would paint over them, taking them in a more abstract, visceral direction. While most were not brilliant works, they were steps along the way to honing her technique and discovering who she was as an artist. One day during a moment of clarity, an earth-shaking realization set in—she suddenly understood how art can heal. From that day on, she knew she would eventually create an art program for people who have gone through the same experience.

"I had a little piece of 'gold' in my pocket that would also help other people. I was going to give this gold to someone else, because it's made me who I am and I wanted to use it to help others."

The small apartment the two lived in provided very little space for the large canvases Masik envisioned. During bad weather they stood in the small hallway off the kitchen, sometimes propped up sideways if too tall to place upright. When the weather was beautiful, work moved outside onto the balcony. Finally her business sense, honed during those early entrepreneurial years, kicked in. A rundown building slated for demolition became available and for three hundred dollars she received permission to use the space. It was in such a bad state structurally that pigeon droppings would fall on the paintings as she worked. With no money for babysitting, her son played at her feet. His handprints would be in the painting if she turned around for even a minute. Everything was incorporated into the final work.

Masik next began to explore different mediums.

"I am the type of artist to take a medium apart, manipulate it, and stretch it to its fullest potential."

This new direction created work that began to catch the

eye of collectors. Slowly pieces began to sell—a painting here, a painting there. She was living totally clean—no drinking or smoking—meditating and writing in a journal. Her spirituality became evident in the canvases and she decided to give them Latin names. Despite an innate shyness, a vision of painting live drew her out of her studio. She first carried her easel to the streets of Vancouver's historic Gastown, to the sidewalk during a local jazz festival; she painted as people walked past. The artist found the in-the-moment feeling of live performance compelling. Next thing you know, a request came to do a twenty-foot canvas live during a concert, and other offers soon followed.

Masik had been selling a bit of her work here and there, but decided it was time to take it to the next level by working on new ways of marketing. First she went to her closest friends. Then she went into her doctor's office. She just showed up with five paintings and said, "So which do you like?" Cold calls with a stack of business cards in hand were the hardest. She didn't know what to say, but the results spoke volumes. The new direction was working.

In 2003, Masik conceived another unique performance piece designed to explore the idea of finding her true self. She built a soundproof box, installed a port-a-potty in the corner, and sealed herself in for five days. Internet viewers vicariously shared the experience through a live feed. It was a form of sensory deprivation that stripped life to its basic elements.

She remembers, "There was a random timer on the light so I lost track of the time. In the beginning, I was trying to grasp onto the normal things we hold onto, but all of these illusions started falling away. I kept a big journal and in it you can see where I'm trying to track time. I lost. I seriously started hallucinating and went a bit nutty. In moments of darkness, I would meditate, sleep, or sculpt. I painted the walls and called it the Fall of the Apple and the Ascension of Man. I had the most monumental experiences of who I was."

It took weeks after coming out of the box to be comfortable in groups. Even colours initially looked surreal. An unexpected side effect was that her ability to express herself artistically exploded. Before this experience she was creating five paintings at once—afterwards, she was working on twenty to thirty at the same time.

Performance art has continued to be an intricate part of Masik's work. In one three-year period alone, she had nineteen live performances commissioned in venues scattered around the world. One memorable invitation was in Shanghai.

"I had this private performance for a star and the next thing I know I'm at the Cultural Embassy. Right there on the spot in front of these delegates, I did eight live painting performances in a row and they hung my work with their massive collection. They were astounded I could express myself that way."

The artist was also honoured to receive an invitation to meet one of China's famous calligraphy artists in his own home. She still cherishes the memories of him holding her hand while trying to teach her this intricate art form.

Despite the financial challenges, Masik decided it was time to create her first solo show. No polite gallery with attendees standing around sipping wine—this would be a performance piece. It took a whole year of hard work to become a reality. With no outside financial support, her workload doubled and tripled. She had paintings to finish and sell now to pay for daily living expenses as well as to finance the upcoming show. Simultaneously, she had to work on creating the new series to be featured. Everything that could be sold was sold—every spare dime set aside.

One crucial element to consider was the venue. Downtown Vancouver offered the Canada Post heritage building with a very unusual feature in its basement—a three-hundred-foot-long bicycle tunnel. The exhibit was inspired by dreams, so she chose to have it open only in the evenings. Paintings were displayed along the dimly lit tunnel and performance artists hid in cubbyholes along the way. As guests moved through the exhibit viewing the collection, actors would step out and re-enact the dreams. Some were frightening and once you started down the tunnel, there was nowhere to go but forward. It was art experienced in a deeply visceral way.

Next came a project that would test her to the limits of her endurance—*The Forgotten*. It would take her to a very dark place and create a controversy that continues to this day. Vancouver, British Columbia, has a seedy area referred to as the DTES (Downtown Eastside). Found here are the disenfranchised—sex trade workers, drug users, those with mental illness, and the impoverished. Crime is a fact of life. From the early 1980s to 2002, over sixty women disappeared from this area—some were murdered, others never found. A full one third of these women were First Nations. In the beginning there was little notice of their disappearance as they had lived on the edge of society. When it finally hit the news, Masik felt the tragedy deeply. That could have been her.

"It was difficult to face *The Forgotten*, as I had to face where I related to them. These women were forgotten and ignored long before they disappeared, because of where they lived. They were judged as inconsequential. They each were someone's mother, daughter, sister, friend, and their lives mattered."

It was time to give them a voice.

Work on *The Forgotten* began in 2005 and it took Masik five years to finish the sixty-nine paintings that make up this series—each approximately eight feet by ten feet. They are intense, emotional portraits. In the beginning, her studio ceiling was so low she had to lay the canvases on their side and paint the images cross-wise. Photographs readily available in the media and on posters were the foundation to build on; she took a different approach for each canvas. Masik wanted the final portraits to be truthful and the subject not sanitized. She envisioned the collection displayed in a large public institution where these women would look down on viewers—turning the viewer into the exhibit.

"I thought it would be a great way to open people's eyes to the idea that we have created a lot of these problems and continue to do so."

Labouring in such a dark space took an emotional toll. Important breaks to work on other collections—*Pond, Requiem,* and *Engagement*—offered the artist both an emotional reprieve from the intensity of working on *The Forgotten*, as well as provided much needed funding to continue this important project. For her, the success of each series was defined by personal satisfaction rather than on the stage of public opinion. Some series sold out immediately and others had only six people show up on the opening night. With increasing success came outside pressure to create commercially driven work, but for Masik every series began with the question, "What do I have to say?" Defining herself as an artist meant choosing to break free from the expectations of others and to not focus on the almighty dollar.

"We get so caught up in the dollar value of things that that becomes more important than where your heart is."

Requiem—a series of dreamy, ethereal abstracts—sold out in one night. It was Masik's first major series using resin, wax, clay, and plaster. The pieces were very layered and explored the idea of her personal journey of letting go and the concept of reprieve. Each painting held a deeply personal meaning. Then there was the *Pond* series.

"I walk at Jericho Beach and know that place so well—the sense of the seasons and reflections in the water. I was absorbed into the light, composition, and feeling of the place. It grounded me."

She decided to explore gallery representation in 2008 with her next release—*Engagement*. In this series she used images of bondage as a metaphor for letting go of what holds you back. The dialogue was struggle, sexuality, and giving one's power away—things every woman has experienced at some point in her life. When the galleries were taken aback by the highly sexual images and censored the show, she was furious! In a fit of anger, she partially covered her canvases with a translucent wash that left only part of the original image exposed. The series launched in Vancouver's Windsor Gallery and, despite the initial censorship, was very successful with collectors, and sold quickly.

The Forgotten drew its funding from the release of the intervening three series, but one increasing expense was studio space. The large number and size of her canvases demanded more area for both work and storage. Her first studio was only fifteen hundred square feet. Then came a larger three thousand square foot space. By the time this series of paintings was finished, a fourteen thousand square foot location was needed to house the collection.

Once she had completed *The Forgotten* in 2010, censorship again reared its ugly head. An exhibit slated to launch *The Forgotten* had to be cancelled due to pressure from social activist groups who felt her depictions of missing and murdered women inappropriate. The series and what it represented was misunderstood—she was misunderstood. As the conflict grew, she was portrayed as a privileged white woman trying to capitalize on these tragedies. Nothing could have been further from the truth. The artist had expected there would be controversy; what surprised her was how much the comments hurt.

The media placed the blame of these sixty-five women's deaths on the perpetrator of the crimes, but Masik knew there was more to the story and hoped *The Forgotten* would help to shed light on the bigger picture.

"These women were forgotten and ignored long before they were gone, because of where they lived. They represent marginalized groups that our society created in the poorest neighbourhoods in North America and here we are judging them and saying they are inconsequential if they die. If it had been a rich neighbourhood, no one would have looked the other way. Because we ignored this there are seventy-seven children without mothers."

While working on *The Forgotten*, Masik decided to help the DTES women in a more tangible way, by sharing that little piece of gold in her pocket—the knowledge that art can heal.

"Giving back is a really important part of my work and inspires me because it makes me feel it's not just all about me. It gives me a deeper purpose and motivates me. The better I do, the more I can contribute. These programs instill a sense of contribution and confidence, and seeing it firsthand is so beautiful."

Her first workshops for DTES women were initially called "The Creative Journey." Women were recruited off the streets to attend an eight-week journey of discovery to find their inner voice through artistic expression. Masik stepped in to guide these women, providing all the supplies and even setting up a gallery show for them to sell their work. The course offered a safe, peaceful haven in their chaotic lives.

Three years later, the successful program is now called "Art for Heart" and has an art therapist on staff, as well as a few course offerings available throughout the year. One exciting development is that some of the first participants have now gone on to become mentors to others. Masik is still supporting Art for Heart by helping to raise necessary funding when budget cuts threaten.

The next series she released was *The Caged Bird*. Built around the theme of censorship that Masik had experienced with both her *Engagement* and *The Forgotten* collections, *The Caged Bird* included a live performance piece called "The Awakening," which first debuted in Vancouver and then was taken to Art Basel 2010 in Miami. This live piece is still one of her favourites.

"It was the first performance in twelve years that I felt I nailed. It was more theatrical. I made a ten-foot, hanging, latex cocoon that I broke out of. I was wearing this very ethereal white dress and had long red hair. As I painted, I talked about finding oneself through the creative voice. That was what 'The Awakening' was all about—my journey."

Back in the studio she found herself working on paintings full of animals and mythological creatures, and the light went on. She realized she had been feeling hunted. "The target has been me and I misunderstood." Although it was originally titled "The Hunted," she changed the final name to *Revelation*, as this collection ended up expanding to have so much more to say. Paintings, drawings, sculptures, a video, a performance piece, and a sound installation were all incorporated into the 2011 exhibition. One particularly thought-provoking selection was a three-minute video showing a young girl first playing with Barbies and then playing with breast implants—a comment on beauty and society.

After the release of *Revelation*, Masik found her life in turmoil. A split with her business partner as well as the failure of a personal relationship hit hard. Her large studio space was slated for demolition forcing a relocation and *The Forgotten* controversy continued. For a year and a half, she chose to pull inward and immerse herself in a new collection. The process of making art is healing. Whether she is happy or sad, full of energy or tired, entering her studio and starting to work gives her a feeling like no other.

"I need to be in the studio, it's an obsession. When I come in the studio and am working, I feel that moment of bliss. I love being here."

Painting, sculpture, writing, music, video, sound installations, and other unique exhibits were woven together in the creation of Masik's next series. It was a massive collection. The artist incorporated recycled objects such as used latex gloves and plumbing wire as well as clay resin into the artwork. A few performance pieces already created were revisited in this new series as she felt they had more to say. Collectors attending were given a map on entering that guided them through the fourteen thousand square foot studio—each step along the way revealing a piece of her journey as an artist.

The next chapter? *Corkscrew Follies*! This time she approached creation in a more immediate way.

"The canvas revealed itself to me as I approached, but I didn't try to make sense of it in the normal way. I was dreaming up all these characters—sometimes surreal, sometimes graffiti-like—and letting them tell me a story."

Eighteen thirty-foot canvases offer fables of love and life twisted around. These are themes she has been exploring throughout her career. While art exhibitions are usually experienced visually, letting the viewer decide what they say, Masik instead chose to offer an insight to her original vision.

"Your interpretation is going to be completely different than mine, so there will be a sound component offering nursery rhymes to tell the story in the voice of a young girl, my inner child."

In April 2013, a project very dear to her heart was completed. Seven years in the making, a film on Masik's journey to create *The Forgotten* and to survive the ensuing controversy debuted at the Hot Docs Canadian International Documentary Festival in Toronto; it was an audience favourite. Called *The Exhibition*, it included footage of her working on the paintings as well as interviews pro and con with family members, media, officers, and social activists raising questions about race, privilege, art, and responsibility. Viewers are left to decide for themselves. Being followed for seven years by a camera crew and having her personal life so exposed was difficult for Masik, but in the end, the only opinion that really mattered was that of her son who accompanied her to the film's debut. His response warmed her heart. "This movie is going to change the world."

Super Channel was also impressed and quickly bought the rights to the film. It is now currently available for subscribers to view. The movie has also gone on to be shown at other film festivals in Chicago, San Francisco, New York City, Norway, and in Salem, where it earned a Journalism Award. The documentary film was nominated for six Leo Awards (celebrating excellence in British Columbia film and television), and won three—Best Direction (Damon Vignale), Editing (Damon Vignale and Daryl Bennett), and Overall Sound (Randy Kiss and Dennis McCormack). This recognition has proved validating for the artist and has worked to bring the story of *The Forgotten* onto the world stage.

Although still working on *Corkscrew Follies*, Masik realized it was time to step back out of the studio and start reconnecting with the world.

"I went very inward for the last year and a half because of all the controversy, but I've come to terms with the fact I need to put myself out there again—personally selling my work and taking it to other cities."

In June 2013, Masik launched her first short-term retail "pop-up shop" in the prestigious York area of Toronto. The shop gave her an opportunity to take her work directly to the developers and collectors in a very visible way. The artist handled every detail from location to press release to shipping to launch in studio.

Selling is an important part of the journey for any artist. Fortunately, Masik began to develop those skills early on. Selling online, at art shows and studio shows, and even in retail pop-up shops have all been a part of her journey. Recently though, she came to the realization that to truly have the time to create the artwork waiting for expression, it is time to let go of the reins. With such a diverse portfolio and subject matter, it is time to focus on the international art world by connecting with agents in New York and overseas.

Looking back, the sheer body of work Masik has already created is astounding, but there is so much more she has to say. Each collection shows growth from the previous one—a new depth to the art, an increasing richness in archetypes, and more elaborate themes. The next few years will see the journey becoming global. With her son on the brink of heading off to university, a five-year plan is in the works that includes her spending time in New York, Paris, Shanghai, Germany, and other international cities where she will live, create new art work, and book live performances. The artist has also written two books that will hopefully reach publication and has launched a new website—ConfessionsOfAnArtist.ca. Although she has had to accept that it may never be seen, Masik still embraces an abiding hope that her censored collection—*The Forgotten*—will one day be allowed to tour.

"The entire purpose behind this collection is and always has been to improve the lives of those in the community. Everyone deserves the right to a dignified life."

Pamela Masik chooses to live a life of authenticity, where she defines success by rejecting the comfortable box the art world would prefer she embrace and creating truthful work that can be uncomfortable. Art is a platform for what she has to say—it is the language she speaks. It has not been an easy journey and the controversy has sometimes proved overwhelming. Her life is also defined by her devotion to her son and her continuing work to improve the lives of forgotten women living on the edge of society. Art, family, charity—all three aspects are tightly woven together into a journey of purpose and discovery.

"Even in the face of challenge, it's important to find the courage to live a life of purpose. When you live a life of purpose and share it with the world, it awakens and inspires others to do the same."

Shane Koyczan

"If you can't see something beautiful in yourself, get a better mirror, look a little closer, stare a little longer."

Poetry. The word is full of imagery. One thinks of romance, dusty old books, and hallowed university halls. Traditional poets rarely achieve media attention and publishers are loathe to print their books, as sales numbers are usually small. But the importance of poetry as a form of expression cannot be denied. Modern enthusiasts have given a new life to the genre by changing how we experience it. Known as Spoken Word or Slam Poetry, this literary form is reaching an enthusiastic, younger audience with its powerful voice, and Shane Koyczan (pronounced "coy zan") is one of the gifted contemporary artists leading the way.

It is no surprise the academic world is reluctant to embrace these poets. Change is a six-letter word that comes slowly to course work heavily invested in years of tradition, but these modern artists are not looking for acceptance or accolades from this world. They are not concerned with old-fashioned labels. Koyczan spoke for many when he shared, "I'm not going to argue with people about what I do. There are academics who say it isn't real poetry and I'm fine with that. I'm not applying for a passport into their literary world."

This new form of poetry has forged a unique path to reach an appreciative audience. Finding a modern way to connect and share with enthusiasts was needed for Spoken Word to take fire. Live performance has now become its trademark, with many competitions offering a platform for these artists to share their work. While traditional publishers are loathe to embrace poetry books of any type, self-publishing—often paired with crowd-funding campaigns—has also helped open doors to a new generation.

Koyczan has embraced both performance and publishing with great success, but it was a YouTube video that took this already recognized artist and made him a household name. "To This Day"—a message of hope for victims of bullying—was a collaborative effort between the poet, a production company, and over eighty freelance animators. It uploaded to YouTube in February 2013 and quickly went viral. Within six months, it had received over ten million views. It now has over fourteen million. His TED Talk performance has garnered almost three million. He set up a "To This Day" website—www.tothisdayproject. com—to offer the lyrics and artist credits, as well as a help page with places to contact for those in crisis. The video's success demonstrates the true power of what a community of like-minded individuals can accomplish when working together. The fact that everyone donated their time to make it happen is phenomenal, a fact the poet is extremely proud of, and one the media often misses.

This artist has several sides. Koyczan's message is personal and his voice is an expressive instrument that carries his words out into the audience. When viewing a live performance, an audience can feel a power and rawness that have a physical impact. The effect is a quieter one in written form, but you still find that same spirit. His poems open a window on how life is experienced—offering messages and stories gleaned from his personal journey. This warmth comes out in his monthly newsletters. They begin with "Hello my darlings," and continue on to share something about his personal journey or career.

He offers another side during an interview. Here you meet the more cerebral artist. He is very friendly, but much more self-contained. Answers are intelligent and thoughtful, but expressed without the same emotional depth and vulnerability. It is a surprise. But if you know his story, this natural reserve makes perfect sense. His young years were not easy.

Koyczan was born and raised in the small town of Yellowknife, Northwest Territories. Both parents were very young and the pregnancy a bit of a scandal. The couple didn't stay together and both left shortly after his birth. Rather than losing their grandson to the system, his grandparents stepped in to provide the stable, loving home he grew up in. They are mom and dad without question. Living in Canada's far North meant summer days were up to twenty hours long—great for kids if they could tolerate the mosquitoes. Winters were the polar opposite, with a mere five hours of sunlight on the shortest day and a biting cold. Those months, kids spent a lot of time indoors. It could prove a lonely, isolating time.

Starting school was a real eye-opener into small town life. The bullying started almost immediately. Why? Because Koyczan was being raised by his grandparents.

"It started with kids knowing for some reason that my parents were gone. Then you'd cry in class and it was like blood in the water. Now you have a target on your back and that's all you are—a dartboard."

There were moments of standing up for himself, including one in kindergarten that got him sent to the principal's office. In response to a mean comment one day, he said the first thing that came to mind—not even really knowing what it meant. The bullies were whatever looked like shit. When the school phoned his grandmother, she wasn't all that upset and he learned a valuable lesson. There were no bad words, only ones that weren't appropriate for every situation. But sometimes they were the only ones that fit.

At home, Koyczan filled his time immersed in books and writing.

"Books were my friends. Escapism really, because I just didn't want to be there. I wanted to be anywhere but there. So I spent a lot of time reading. I liked all kinds of books—was a big fan of Roald Dahl in particular. It's funny because you consume all his children-based work and then discover he has more adult fiction that is really interesting."

Watching films in the local theatre offered another great outlet, although his grandparents always worried if he went alone. He had a few friends along the way, but they came from different schools, which made it easier. Socially, school continued to be tough and avoidance became the goal. "When trouble starts, you learn to live in the periphery. You sort of walk in the spaces where they can't see you."

Around the age of fourteen to fifteen, change was in the air. His grandparents retired and moved the family south to Penticton, British Columbia—a larger city and hopefully a new beginning. Koyczan found himself really excited.

"It was amazing. I would get to reinvent myself and start over in a place where nobody knew me. I felt very hopeful at that time in my life."

Unfortunately, the bullying started to happen all over again. A big kid for his age, he finally started to fight back. Ironically this earned him the label of bully from the school counsellor. Feeding this image at least encouraged the bullies to steer clear, but it was also very isolating in its own way. Now Koyczan knew bullying from both sides of the fence—victim and perpetrator. These experiences would eventually provide the inspiration for his first prose novel, *Stickboy*.

Here is an excerpt from *Stickboy*: "I was never meant to be this thing. But it's how I learned to survive. It was my reason my 'because.'"

School did offer some positives in the classroom. English, history, and any type of art offered the most appeal. Writing in particular was Koyczan's overall favourite—it gave him an opportunity to shine. Mostly he wrote short fiction stories with a humorous bent. There was a method to the madness in that being funny might gain some laughs out of the class and perhaps work to ease things up.

"I find people have defense mechanisms in school. You

find whatever you can to get some level of acceptance. If you can make them laugh ..."

Problem-solving labs in science class were also a favourite as they challenged him to find creative solutions. One project assigned after the Exxon Valdez oil spill in 1989 still stands out in his memory.

"In science class that week we had a project where the teacher came in with a tub of water and poured oil on it. We had to figure out a way to get all the oil off safely. There were kids pouring bottles of Joy dish soap in there and all the oil would go to the side, but then we realized there were new chemicals in the water."

Life stepped in during his last few years of high school to give that first firm nudge down the path to Spoken Word Poetry. The drafting class he had signed up for was overbooked. Drafting was a comfort class as it was solitary work. You sit at your desk and draw lines. The school bumped him to the next class available alphabetically and that was Drama. With no social skills and inept at talking with other students, Koyczan felt his life was over. He was wrong. The change was a blessing in disguise.

"We started doing school plays and dinner theatre, which allowed me to be somebody else completely on stage. It helped me in terms of talking to people as they were finally engaging me on a human level."

Here his childhood love of film was reborn. It also offered a supportive social grouping to be a part of, an extra-curricular activity, and a chance to excel.

Koyczan's first drama teacher forced him from the

shadows by demanding participation. It was just what he needed. "I was the guy sitting in the class not wanting to play any of the reindeer games." The second teacher built on that foundation with a more nurturing touch. In fact, she was the first to take a chance on him by giving him the lead role as Edward Llewellyn in *The Attempted Murder of Peggy Sweetwater*. His initial reaction was not positive, but that quickly changed opening night.

"At first I was cast in a minor role, because I didn't participate very well in the theatre games. Then I did a bang up job and she moved me to the bigger role saying, 'I think you can carry it.' I was terrified. It was a long play. Who wants that responsibility as a kid—memorizing all those lines? But the role was a confidence builder. It was absolutely amazing to go out on stage and hear people laugh at what I was saying or doing. Being on stage led to the burgeoning of my own confidence."

After high school, the future poet headed off to university to study Political Science—a strange choice given his love of theatre. Why? Koyczan was, and still is, passionate about politics; he felt he could make a difference. It was also a position of power to work from. But life again stepped in to point him in a new direction, this time in the form of a professor who noticed the talent apparent in his class essays. The professor's encouragement to take a serious look at transferring to the Creative Writing Program would drastically alter Koyczan's future. By the start of second semester, he had changed his courses to accommodate the new choice of studies and he was commuting with fellow students to the Kelowna campus.

Literary professor Nancy Holmes took a personal interest in this young writer who was producing overly dramatic, incomplete novels filled with Byronic heroes. She encouraged him to try his hand at shorter works that would be easier to finish. Around the same time, Holmes offered a workshop called "The Poetry Sweat Shop." Here students were challenged to create poetry quickly on random subjects and present them orally to the rest of the class.

"There were a bunch of subjects on pieces of paper in a hat. Everyone would reach in and pull out a subject—I think mine was something like mashed potatoes. You had about a half hour to write your poem and then had to get up and read it out loud. This was the first time I had ever read a poem out loud." He was hooked.

Koyczan and his friend Matt decided to start a poetry reading night at a coffee shop called The Hog's Breath in Penticton, British Columbia. It started as an Open Mic Poetry Night and then became an Open Mic. There was nothing like it in the area and the event quickly grew in popularity. Even after he moved away, another enthusiast stepped in to run it for several years until the lease for the space was purchased by Starbucks. Unfortunately, Open Mic Night never found a new home; it was relegated to history.

Near the end of his second year, Koyczan sat down with two valued professors—Nancy Holmes and John Lent—to discuss his future. The question on his mind was what was the best path to pursue as a writer. Their honest advice struck a chord.

"You don't have to wait until you are done here. If this is really something you want to do, just get out there and do it. A degree isn't going to help. You need to find a mecca and look for that subculture. It's out there."

That was all the encouragement he needed. The next step for Koyczan to pursue his passion was a move to Vancouver and, with all funds exhausted, poverty—subsisting on a bag of rice, working odd security jobs, and when all else failed, surviving for a short time on welfare. Trying to make a living writing was a tough road. Where would the money come from? He didn't have a good answer, but did discover it was easier to get a gig performing his own material than a job writing for someone else.

The move from written to oral poetry was natural for Koyczan, although he has always offered work in both styles. "Some of what I wrote I felt warranted oral performance; others felt more page-driven." Vancouver's Poetry Slams offered him a chance to try out new material and hone his performance skills. Being a part of this subculture also offered a welcome community of like-minded individuals. What is a good slam?

"There is a saying in Slam, 'The points are not the point, the point is the poetry,' and that's very true. Good slams are where the audience is enthusiastic. Even if you get a three out of ten, people still appreciate the fact you went up there. What matters is that people get excited about poetry."

Poetry Slams are judged by a focus group of their peers so at each competition, five judges are selected from the audience. Koyczan's strong performances led to participation in big, sometimes international events. At the US Poetry Slam Competition in 2000, he beat over two hundred and fifty competitors to become the first winner from outside the US. Some of his other wins include the CBC Poetry Face-Off and what he calls the "Canadian Spoken Word Olympics"—The Canadian Festival of Spoken Word. As he continued to hone his craft, the list of accolades and opportunities to perform grew.

The National Poetry Association held its 25th Anniversary Celebration at the Masonic Temple in San Francisco in 2000. This benefit—called "Celebration of the Word"—offered a rare appearance by legendary author, Maya Angelou. Seven others were also listed in the evening's program, including "National Poetry Slam Champion Shane Koyczan," and fellow artists Ariana Waynes and James Cagney. That evening is still one of Koyczan's favourite performances, because it was where he had the privilege of meeting Angelou.

"It was pretty memorable. We got ushered into a room one at a time to meet her. I didn't know what to say so I asked her, 'How do you stay beautiful?' She laughed. Ariana, James, and I read before her. When she got on stage, she said, 'The future of poetry is in good hands.' It was amazing."

Being a spoken word poet requires booking a gig and that means being on the road. Touring became a constant during this time and the Greyhound bus his means of transport. It was "couch surfing across America" at its best.

There was no agent handling his schedule and very little money paid for bookings. Most only covered his bus fare to the next city where hopefully they would offer to feed him. The payback was getting to follow his passion, meeting many amazing people, and seeing some incredible performances. Melding music to his poetry added a new dimension to his performances, as well as a chance to tour with fellow artists.

In 2003, Koyczan formed Tons of Fun University (TOFU) with American poet Mighty Mike McGee and, several months later, fellow Canadian poet C.R. Avery. Invitations from literary events and folk festivals added to his already large number of solo bookings—over two hundred in some years. Then in 2006, he joined forces with a new group for a single performance. Billed as "Shane Koyczan and the Short Story Long"—the show garnered rave reviews and they soon found themselves on a British Columbia wide tour. There was a chemistry here that struck a chord. Although a few members have changed over the years, the group is still performing together and have several recordings to their credit. "Working with these artists is a great growing experience. I just do the spoken work and leave the hard work to the musicians."

He met many unique people when he was on tour. In the end, some of the most interesting turned out to be just everyday individuals. One in particular still stands out.

"I was on a gig in Fayetteville, Arkansas, and went down to the lobby. There was a hockey game on and I was just sitting there when this guy sits down next to me and starts telling his story. At first, I just wanted to be left alone. But the more I started listening, the more I realized this guy had something he needed to tell someone."

This man prepared the final meals for death row inmates. One of the inmates currently awaiting execution had killed a law enforcement officer—the man's own brother! It was a huge moral dilemma. This conversation struck Koyczan profoundly and provided inspiration for his poem

"Restaurant" *(an excerpt)*

> *I met a man who makes meals at a restaurant*
> *where there's no menu*
> *but everything's on it*
> *impossible*
> *I know*
> *but I met a man who makes meals at a restaurant*
> *called death row*
> *I met a man who makes the last meals*
> *and I know way too many people*
> *who would attack him asking him how it feels*
> *to be part of something like that*
> *so instead we just chew the fat*
> *and I listen.*

It quickly became apparent extra money could be made after performances if he had something to sell. With no finances in place to publish a traditional book, Koyczan used photocopiers for a pay-as-you-go option. He produced tons of small "magazines" as he crisscrossed the country—seven poems in a "book" of photocopied pages stapled together for just three dollars.

The very first time he did this was when he was invited to perform the sponsorship poem at the Vancouver Writers Festival. He was the only unpublished writer the festival had ever included, and remembers, "I was in the lobby stapling my little handmade books together and the writers were walking by, laughing at me. 'What does this kid think he's doing?' These incredible writers that I loved were all there with their nicely made books. It was so weird because, after I performed, I sold everything I brought. It was very validating."

His strong performance at the event made important people—including publishers—suddenly take notice, but the traditional route to releasing his first book just didn't feel like the right choice. Instead, Koyczan chose to self-publish.

He released *Visiting Hours*—his first full-length collection of poetry—in 2005. The literary world was curious to see what this young talent—mostly known for his spoken word performances—could bring to the table. They were not disappointed. The book offered a collection of over thirty poetry/spoken word pieces that looked at our very humanity—weaving the uncomfortable, the sad, and the funny occurrences in our everyday lives into powerful words full of imagery. The book opens with a heartfelt acknowledgment of the people who have touched his life in a positive way.

"For the teachers who have been my friends. For the

friends who have been my family. For the family whom I love."

This volume of poetry earned the distinction of becoming the only book of any genre selected that season by both the *Guardian* (UK) and *The Globe and Mail* for their annual Best Book of the Year lists. *Visiting Hours* has since gone on to have three published editions including a new e-book offering additional content. He was invited to perform at the Edinburgh International Book Festival in 2005 where *The Scotsman* newspaper noted that his was the best poetry reading of the event.

The next few years held many firsts as his résumé expanded at an incredible rate. Koyczan was now a triple threat—television, print, and live performance. Bravo Canada featured him in their season two opening episode of *Heart of a Poet*. On the literary front was the release of his second book, *Stickboy*. This novel in prose offers the reader a glimpse into the effects of bullying—if you keep poking something with a stick it will eventually turn around and bite you.

It wasn't originally meant for publication. "I was just writing it for myself. Sometimes writing is therapy and I needed to get it out of my system."

The project of writing *Stickboy* changed several times. It was going to be a graphic novel, then a regular novel, and then ended up as a novel in verse. A lot of thought went into the final version.

"The book is quite thick. If students, especially troubled kids, see a thick book, they think it's going to take a long time to read and they're not going to want to get through it. When you open this book up, it's in poetry format so there's not a lot of words on the page. As thick as the book is, it's a quick read. For them to get through something this big is quite rewarding."

Canadian Tourism offered the poet a commission to perform an original work at the July 1, 2007, Canada Day festivities on Parliament Hill in Ottawa. His offering—"We Are More"—struck a strong emotional chord with the audience that day. The poem gives a nod to world stereotypes, the country's youth, and Canada's potential as a nation. The message is that Canada deserves to be embraced with pride.

"I was just telling people we're more than what the world thinks of us. We're more than the brunt of a joke. We're more than clichés put on us by other countries. Canada has been, for a long time, viewed as a funny neighbour. That's beautiful. Those small differences are what make us so lovable."

Three years later he was invited to perform "We Are More" at the opening ceremonies for the 2010 Vancouver Winter Olympics. Accepting the invitation was not an easy decision for the poet. On one hand, it was a huge opportunity as it would be the largest stage Spoken Word Poetry had ever been a part of. An enormous international television audience would also tune in. On the other hand, lines were being drawn by the art community over concerns about interference—Koyczan was worried he would be criticized for participating. In the end, he answered yes, but he had some anxious moments. One was working on the elevated platform, as he is terrified of heights. Right before curtain time, the enormity of the moment hit. There would be an estimated 3.5 billion people watching him world-wide. Blocking out all distractions meant focusing on the message.

"What I do before I read any poem to any audience is try to remember—to step back into the place where I wrote it in the first place. It allows me to connect to it on an emotional level."

"We Are More" (an excerpt)

> *but we are more*
> *than genteel or civilized*
> *we are an idea in the process*
> *of being realized*
> *we are young*
> *we are cultures strung together*
> *then woven into a tapestry*
> *and the design*
> *is what makes us more*
> *than the sum total of our history*
> *we are an experiment going right for a change.*

Koyczan's next work—*Our Deathbeds Will be Thirsty* —was performed live on stage at the Vogue Theatre in Vancouver to rave reviews. This collection of fifty-one poems ranges in length from the very short "Patriot" to longer verses such as "I Am A Kid." They invite us to take a look at our lives, our interactions with those around us, and the way we looked at ourselves as we grew up. In "Remember How We Forgot," he encourages us to "live and remember ... burn as if you were an ember ... capable of starting fires ... like each moment inspires the next...."

"To This Day"—destined to create a ripple worldwide through its video release—was a part of this collection.

Koyczan had no desire to revisit his difficult school years. They were best left behind. But, his grandmother had kept all the books he had written over the years and handed them over one day. First they sat ignored, collecting dust; then curiosity got the upper hand.

"I cracked open a book and started reading. I realized in the middle of all that darkness there was still somebody there and moments of beauty and levity that shone through. Certainly there were dark times, but my childhood wasn't just that. I wasn't joyless."

It was a revelation. While reading those early journals, the concept for "To This Day" began to emerge. It proved personally cathartic, but also gave a voice and hope to many others who felt alone and powerless. "My experience with violence in schools still echoes throughout my life, but standing to face the problem has helped me in immeasurable ways."

The poem shines a light on the long-term impact bullying can have by giving us three powerful examples including Koyczan's. As with all of his work, the poem starts at the end. "I write backwards so I know my ending before I start the beginning. Then I needed something that humanized me. The pork chop story was perfect. It's a silly story that is also kind of sad. Next, I started looking at stories of other people who were walking in the periphery. There were so many verses originally. I could have gone on forever."

In the end, highlighting just three stories kept the focus tight and the message clear. Bullying starts with words that paint a target on your back. These words are profoundly destructive and have a lasting effect.

Koyczan nurtured the idea of turning "To This Day" into an animated video—offering the message to a wider audience that the victims of bullying are not alone. To let them know they are not alone. To give them a voice. There are tons of us who have gone through the same thing. There is hope. Turning this idea into a reality all started with a pro bono project for the Dalai Lama Centre in Vancouver. Giant Ant—the project's developers—needed someone to do the voice-over and he was already in the studio working on another project for them. A deal was struck.

"I said yes based on the idea we could do a trade of talent down the road and the studio do a little something for me. Down the road eventually came. We came up with the idea of doing a social call out for animation. Then we started dividing up the video into twenty-second segments. The animators were all working blindly from one another. It was a real project to be a part of and, to me, the important part about it, which the media sort of glazed over, was the fact that nobody got paid. Everyone did it because they knew somebody or they themselves had been through it.

They could see it was worthwhile and that meant a lot to me."

In the end, over four hundred animators submitted clips of which eighty-six were used in the final video.

"To This Day" (excerpt)

*I'm not the only kid
who grew up this way
surrounded by people who used to say
that rhyme about sticks and stones
as if broken bones
hurt more than the names we got called
and we got called them all
so we grew up believing no one
would ever fall in love with us
that we'd be lonely forever
that we'd never meet someone
to make us feel like the sun
was something they built for us
in their tool shed
so broken heart strings bled the blues
as we tried to empty ourselves
so we would feel nothing
don't tell me that hurts less than a broken bone*

The video also caught the attention of TED Talks. The organization had approached him before, but only to do a poetry reading. This time they were offering him the chance to talk with the audience. There were only two snags. The next conference was in only five days, which left him little time to prepare, and he was sick with the flu the day of the performance. In the end, it all came together. Koyczan's years of experience helped him dig deep as he presented a five-minute opening piece that led seamlessly into a performance of "To This Day."

"I really wanted to lull people into it. Here is a bit of back story—a bit of my story—and here's why I'm here talking about it. I was very happy with the response. There was an incredible group of people and such a great community. It was like you've been through the forest and you find your tribe. The audience was filled with people who maintained who they were despite everything and it felt like many of them had been through what I had been through."

Those listening were deeply moved and offered a standing ovation. Tears were in evidence. The only downside was the loss of his voice immediately after he left the stage. His body had been pushed as far as it would go. All he could do when congratulated was smile.

Koyczan has moved firmly out of the shadows of performance artist and author for Spoken Word aficionados and into the global spotlight where his words reach a much wider audience. The world has officially taken notice. Thompson Artist Management is now on board to help with bookings. Time must be allotted for interviews and personal appearances in addition to solo and band performances. His website—www.shanekoyczan.com—has taken on a new look and features his bio, an online store, a monthly poem for all subscribers, and an appearance dates page. Email subscribers receive a monthly letter with personal notes about his journey.

Success has brought welcome new avenues to explore. The poet was offered an opportunity by the Vancouver Opera to work as a librettist on an opera version of *Stickboy*, with the goal of possibly taking the production to the Sundance Festival. This innovative work opened at the Queen Elizabeth Theatre in Vancouver on October 23, 2014. Koyczan hopes the subject matter will help this art form speak to a younger generation. Another new venture will be a future collaboration with a live symphony orchestra to create *Stations of the Heart*. He has also written and starred in two commercials and had his video poem, "Instructions For A Bad Day," showcased at the 2012 Vancouver Film Festival.

A Bruise On Light—Koyczan's third major book of poetry—was released in August 2014. This collection was self-published with the support of a Kickstarter Campaign. His fanbase is large and responded enthusiastically by pledging over six times the amount needed. In return they were rewarded with everything from thanks, to signed copies of the book, to tickets for live performances, to a romantic poem for your special someone read over the phone on Valentine's Day. Although his subject matter is often serious, there is a fun side that peaks out from time to time. His promotion for this campaign included the comment, "Don't let the word poetry scare you ... it'll be rad. I mention blobfish in it."

Some things have not changed. Writing is still a passion that consumes up to five hours a day. His implements are varied—laptop, typewriter, and pen. Family and friends are always on hand to offer a welcome wake-up call if they see changes coming from his new celebrity status. His mother came back into his life—a difficult journey that took him through his anger at her abandonment and helped him in some measure to let go of the past.

Koyczan still wrestles with his experiences of being bullied. In one monthly email, he shared this insight. "I grew up very angry, and had difficulty understanding where those feelings came from. Some instances were easier to decipher than others; parental abandonment factored into my life heavily, and gave the people around me an easy button to push. Other moments were subtler and took a tremendous amount of searching to find the root cause ... I haven't answered all my questions yet, and I'm not even sure the answers I do have are the right ones ... but I've found solace in attempting to understand myself."

Koyczan's definition of success is as down to earth as they come. It has changed from being defined by a goal to being something much more—a way of living.

"Success is such a weird creature. For the first five years you're just doing stuff for free, hoping someone might buy a book or whatever. I'd say I felt successful the first time someone offered me a paid gig. More than anything else, I get to do what I love to do and I make a living at it. I'm not saying it's George Clooney success, but I can go see a movie when I want to. That's success."

Lisa-Marie Mazzucco

"There are moments in your life where, if that moment didn't happen, the rest of your life would have taken a totally different direction."

The last decade has seen an amazing new trend grow by leaps and bounds—rebranding. This is especially true of women. While there has been great progress, women still often hold down the fort when it comes to house and family. At the same time, they have moved out of the home and exerted an incredible influence on all industries. It can be a tough balancing act. So it comes as no surprise that, as their kids get more independent, women move into new careers that offer greater personal satisfaction and new and interesting challenges. Lisa-Marie Mazzucco is one such woman.

What do we want in terms of female role models for our young women? Confidence, a willingness to work hard for what she wants, thinking outside the box, a love of learning, creativity, balance in life, and curiosity—Lisa-Marie embraces them all. While the first part of her professional journey was closely intertwined with her husband's, world-renowned fashion photographer and artist Raphael Mazzucco, the second half went in a new direction entirely of her own doing. And she loves it. It is solo, fully hers creatively, and done on her own terms. The journey from childhood to this moment has been full of interesting twists and turns, but life for this multitalented woman is for embracing fully, and each step along the way is just one more piece in the puzzle. The final picture is yet to be completed.

Lisa-Marie was born in Nova Scotia, but raised in British Columbia from the age of four by a single mum who was determined to offer her all the opportunities she had never had. One early trademark that is still true today is Lisa-Marie's enthusiasm. Well, that plus drive and talent. Every activity was a great activity.

"My mother enrolled me in figure skating, ballet, gymnastics, and piano lessons, figuring I would choose one that I would stick with. She didn't count on me loving all of them and not wanting to quit. She ended up working four jobs to support it all. At the time, I was totally unaware of her sacrifice."

Lisa-Marie excelled in most, which didn't help. Fortunately, figure skating finally rose to the top. She spent four to eight hours a day practising at the local rink. At the age of fourteen, she earned her first gold medal for Canada in that year's Commonwealth Games. Although ice-skating continued to take precedence throughout her high school years, she did not abandon all her early passions totally. Even today, she stills enjoys playing the piano.

Another interest that would prove to be key in her future was make-up. Experimentation began early and by grade seven, she was doing all the make-up for the school play. This talent received an extra boost when, a few years after graduating high school, the chance arose to work as a model in Tokyo. Back then, the field was more wide open in terms of looks and it was exciting for the twenty-year-old Lisa-Marie to head off on this international adventure. She spent three years working in Japan while soaking up as much as she could about the fashion industry—the logistics of photo shoots, make-up, modelling, and styling.

"I have to say, in all my travels, I have never been to a place quite like Tokyo. It's truly amazing. It was also as frustrating as hell. I was going nonstop the whole time I was there and not a day went by when I wasn't in tears over something. But it is an incredible place and the great experiences I had there are too numerous to mention."

After three years she decided to head home to Vancouver. Lisa-Marie is the type of person who thrives on being busy and is quickly bored, so it wasn't long before she found jobs on both sides of the camera—a make-up artist here, a model there. One of the first photographers she collaborated with was preparing models to head to Japan. Her experience and intimate knowledge of the Asian market proved a tremendous asset. Then a new door opened. Only two weeks after returning home she met an up-and-coming photographer who would change her life—Raphael Mazzucco. It was instant chemistry. First they collaborated on one shoot. Then they decided to start working together on several shoots and began dating at the same time. Not long after, he dropped a bomb. He was heading off to Milan to live and work. She responded, "I'm coming, too."

Their home in Milan was a small seven-hundred-square-foot apartment. It was here that make-up changed from an interest to a full-time job, but her responsibilities grew to encompass much, much more. Lisa-Marie first took care of all the models' styling, hair, and make-up, and then headed off to the kitchen table to do post-production work on completed film (this was the pre-digital camera era). Raphael would head into the bedroom to push the furniture out of the way so it could be used as a studio. After he finished photographing the models, he would move to the kitchen to cook the dinner while she finished processing the film.

There was a rhythm and synergy to their day that worked well and both admit they learned a lot about their several crafts. Preconceived notions were abandoned as they allowed themselves to explore, to be spontaneous, to adapt, and to find their own voices as artists. One surprise was the power of mistakes. "We would notice the mistakes were sometimes the most beautiful part of the actual image—like whether the edge of the film was clipped or a bit of light got in."

In the beginning, they built their portfolio by testing models for local agencies here and there, but a random phone call changed everything almost overnight. Raphael answered the phone one day to discover it was a well-known Italian photographer looking for someone else—a wrong number! Instead of hanging up, Raphael continued to talk to the caller for over an hour. The Italian photographer not only introduced the couple to agencies and personal clients all over Italy, but went on to become one of their closest friends with whom they are still in contact today. Over the next three years the couple worked nonstop, producing up to six shoots a day and became well-known in particular for their stunning beauty shots.

Life was moving along well. Lisa-Marie was settled in Milan, enjoying her work and had just flown home to Vancouver for a short visit, when she discovered she was expecting. They were both absolutely thrilled. She found a doctor on returning to Italy and nesting quickly ensued. Walls were painted. Nursery furniture purchased. Her life seemed to be on a predictable path, but change was in the air. One month before their son Sascha was due to be born, a great offer from a magazine in Amsterdam came in that was too good to pass up. The couple quickly packed their belongings and headed off to Holland. On arrival the priorities were first home, next an obstetrician, and then it was right back to work.

In Amsterdam their professional careers took on a new dimension. Each had a separate agent who handled their bookings. There were still many jobs where they worked together, but opportunities also arose to take on independent shoots that interested them personally and offered new artists to collaborate with. Lisa-Marie worked throughout her entire pregnancy and headed back not long after Sascha was born. She remembers, "I didn't have babysitters, I didn't have a nanny, I didn't have family, and I was breastfeeding. So I would just put him in his Snuggly Baby Carrier and he would be on my back all day while I worked."

Not all was smooth sailing. When Sascha was seven months old, they needed to find a new apartment. Raphael signed the lease before Lisa-Marie had even seen it and, although it's a funny memory now, she was not happy back them.

"There were about twenty cement stairs to climb that were so steep I needed two hands to hold the railing. There was an open wood-burning stove on the floor in the middle of the living room that was the main heat source. A second stove was upstairs in our bedroom right next to the bed. Part of the second floor was missing, so it was a sheer drop to the first floor if you didn't know beforehand. There were hanging wires that would shock you if you touched them. It was basically a tear-down and no place for a child. I tethered Sascha up to the ceiling with a huge bungee cord attached to his Jolly Jumper and he lived in it until bedtime every night to keep him safe."

Needless to say, they only stayed there three months while they searched for a safer home.

When Sascha was only four months old, the Mazzuccos returned to Vancouver for a visit. One day, a random thought arose. Why don't we get married—now? And so they did. Raphael's dad let them know there was a woman close by who could handle the ceremony and license—they should go talk to her—and then added, "Oh, by the way, there is a sale on corn on the cob. Do you mind picking a bag up on the way here?" It was that casual.

The next day the whole ceremony took five minutes with only Sascha and Raphael's parents in attendance. The couple wore their best jeans. The one photo taken was a poor one snapped while they were signing the marriage certificate—a surprising note considering they both worked in the industry. On the weekend the real fun began. Their marriage was the best excuse ever to throw a huge party for all their friends and local family. They even had a singer perform live. Reality hit when Lisa-Marie phoned her mother in Halifax to give her the good news. It was not well-received as her mother wanted to have been there most of all. She was also very religious and had hoped for a proper Catholic church wedding.

Not long after the couple returned to Amsterdam, they received a new offer to consider—this time in Montreal. It was an important move as it was taking them ever closer to the goal they had set long ago when they had left for Milan—to eventually live and work in New York City. For Raphael in particular, that meant arriving with an excellent photographic portfolio that would attract an agent. They continued to work in Montreal both as a team and on separate assignments such as with *Elle Canada*, Parasuco Jeans, and Buffalo Jeans. Two years later, it felt like the right time to take a leap of faith and make the move they had been working toward, but it proved to be much more difficult than they expected.

It was now do or die, so the pressure was on. The Mazzuccos had to borrow money from their family just to get started in this expensive city. Then they were given only one week to get out of their first rental and move into a new home that was as yet just a pipe dream as rental properties were extremely scarce. The process hit a serious blimp with Lisa-Marie smack dab in the middle. This mistake, however, ended up being a blessing in disguise. She was supposed to drop off a cheque to their new landlord, but missed him and lost the apartment. Raphael was upset. She was upset, as well as feeling ultimately responsible.

"'That's it, we're going to have to leave New York and it's all my fault.' I was crying and carrying on. Then I remembered there was another place we hadn't seen yet. There was no electricity, no bathroom, and no kitchen. We went to see it in the middle of the night. It was the whole floor of a building, but it was gutted office space and it was dark. We just walked around feeling the walls and said, 'We'll take it.' After moving in, we found out the man upstairs was a talent agent who had just lost his photographer of twenty years. He and Raphael met, decided to work together, and this man is still his agent today. If I had not lost that first apartment ... I still think about that moment."

Sascha was now an active two-year-old. Lisa-Marie felt it was the right time to take a step back from the crazy life and enjoy a quieter pace, but first she had to break the news to her husband. Her words were simple. "I don't want to be a make-up artist with you, because I can't do two-week trips all the time. That's why I'm quitting." He understood completely and accepted her decision. A new world now opened up that offered her the free time she craved to enjoy being with Sascha. She kept busy, but the nomadic lifestyle and frenetic schedule were put behind her.

Raphael's career took off and travelling to shoot at locations around the world became an increasing reality. Sometimes he was gone for months at a time. She would still step in occasionally to help Raphael when he was in town working on a local project, or take the odd freelance assignment, but she chose to have no agent.

Lisa-Marie loved being a full-time mum and has many fond memories of one-on-one time with her son.

"I remember Sascha was about six when the Harry Potter video game came out. One night we were playing against each other. We were at the part where you have to play quidditch and were so into it that we couldn't stop. Neither of us could manage to win. Raphael ended up having to eat dinner without us."

This close relationship continued all through Sascha's teen years. One time, she flew with him and his friends to Pittsburgh during spring break to attend the concert of a heavy metal band they both liked: Avenged Sevenfold. Long story short—she was the one who ended up crowd surfing all the way to the stage that night. "Fun times!"

By the time Sascha was six and in school full time, the easily bored Lisa-Marie needed a new challenge. After working behind the scenes on so many photo shoots over the years—wearing the multiple hats of make-up artist, hair stylist, set designer, wardrobe stylist, film processor, printer, spotter, and retoucher—she decided maybe it was time to try looking through the lens and depressing the shutter. Raphael, always supportive, stepped in to pick out the camera and then gave her room to explore.

This was only the beginnings of the digital era, so her first camera was a completely manual 35mm Nikon. There was an instant chemistry when she held it the first time. "There was no learning curve for me. I had been doing everything except this for years. I was so integrated into it that holding the camera just felt like a non-event. I felt like a photographer after the first shoot."

Lisa-Marie's initial goal was just to make a little side money and feel more productive, to have her own artistic career. She remembers, "I wasn't sure if it would work out or not, but once I started shooting, it was a pretty quick transition and I was busy almost immediately. It was just meant to be. I didn't want the same career as my husband, as I was done with the travelling and didn't want to start doing that all over again. So I steered my career toward portraiture instead of fashion."

Having made the decision to not embrace the fashion photographer lifestyle, she had to decide what direction to take. Lisa-Marie was looking for a quiet space where her creativity and talents could find the perfect outlet. She began with children and actors she met through Sascha's school. Then there was a singer in her building who need-ed someone to take her first shots. It wasn't long before she was on the path to specializing in photographing classical musicians.

The first classical musician she photographed found her website through an internet search. Her name, Angela Jia Kim. Although this musician has since moved on to become an entrepreneur with her own skin care line—Om

Aroma & Co.—back then she was a concert pianist. Lisa-Marie ended up shooting all Kim's promotion pictures as well as her album cover. She went on to shoot this pianist three or four times over her career. Kim also passed on Lisa-Marie's name to another classical client, The Albers Trio, who quickly booked their own shoot.

One of the things Lisa-Marie learned early on was not to touch the instruments. It was a lesson she would never forget. "Soovin Kim was my first violinist. I didn't know much about classical instruments. I played the piano and that's pretty sturdy. We were shooting on the beach and back then I didn't work with an assistant, so was on my own. I had my camera, my bag, my hair and make-up stuff around my waist—I'm doing everything. I needed him to get up on this big rock to do this silhouette photo. I said, 'Here, I'll hold your violin while you get up on the rock.' He gently gave it to me and I didn't think twice. I stuck it between my knees so I could hold my camera. He went pure white. I swear to God right there on the spot. The earth stood still for a moment. His violin was worth five million dollars and I had it just sitting between my knees."

Fortunately, all was forgiven and she went on to shoot him three more times. This was not the only shoot with an expensive instrument. Another one featured Anne Akiko Meyers. Her violin was originally owned by Napoleon and was named Molly. Now she just tells her subjects to get their instruments and lets them take full charge of them.

There are challenges to shooting non-models that are just a part of the job. Fortunately, all her work behind the scenes processing film prepared her for the task. These are real people, with real bodies who do not spend their days working out or dieting. They spend their days practising for their next performance or recording session. Most are often terribly insecure in front of the camera, which means a photographer needs to find just the right approach to help them relax.

Photoshop is an important part of post-production. The photographer wants to make very subtle adjustments that will only polish the final photo without changing the look too drastically. This is not an easy task and one that is a true balancing act. The editing process often ends up taking the most time on any new assignment. It is also the most difficult part for Lisa-Marie as she doesn't have a lot of patience with sitting. But it is important, so she makes it happen. In gratitude, some of her clients have dubbed her "Doctor Lisa."

The other beauty of this new direction was the freedom. Her husband is often working on sets with tons of people swirling around. He has to find a way to block all the distractions and find that quiet space where the magic can occur. Then there is the need to work within a client's vision and travelling constantly is a given. The upside—fame.

For Lisa-Marie, she was first of all a make-up artist and that didn't usually draw a lot of media attention; she is perfectly fine with not being a public figure. Then there was the desire to work with more control and in a quieter space. While working with professional musicians, she is one hundred percent in charge of concept, styling, make-up, hair, and post-production. Although she has now added an assistant to help her on set, in the beginning it was just her alone with her client and the occasional agent along for the ride. It's a perfect match for her vision and experience.

"There is no art director breathing down my neck. When I see the sheer number of people Raphael has to deal with on one shoot, I feel spoiled. But there is no fame in what I do. I often sit home in my pyjamas and work. It's great. And I love my clients."

Lisa-Marie's photographic style has stayed fairly consistent over her career—romantic and classical. It's one that works well given who she works with—Yi-Jia Susanne Hou, Anne Akiko Myers, The Emerson Quartet, Simone Dinnerstein, Zuill Bailey, and Grammy winner Joshua Bell, to name a few. The settings chosen and the colours used when retouching all work together to create this aesthetic.

"I am very girlie with my photography. I can only be edgy to a certain degree because of my clientele. Sometimes I'll go a little more edgy, but I'll use those photos for my site or for the artist's personal use."

Her portfolio came to the attention of Sony Records and she has since produced covers for several of their artists over the last few years. But in the end, she doesn't really consider herself an artist. She just enjoys the process.

"As much as I have all these creative jobs, I don't find myself a really creative person. But I can do anything. You give me something to do, or copy, or make, and I'll do it. I don't pick up a camera unless I'm working, I just don't. But I can do it, do it well, and people like my work."

How does a new shoot begin? Usually it starts when she receives an email from a potential client. Most have already seen many of their colleagues on her website and love their photos. What they want are rates and availability. Once the process has begun, it moves along a pretty predictable path.

"They all have concert gowns and tuxedos—lots of them, all custom made—so clothing is not an issue. They bring fabulous stuff and I have a lot of accessories, so we work it out. As for a concept, sometimes we talk beforehand, but other times I don't do that until I'm sitting with them and see what they have brought in terms of clothes. I do their hair and make-up, see their character, and then I shoot."

In 2002, an unexpected change of residence simplified her life and work even more. The family moved three hours outside New York City to a house in Montauk. It wasn't planned. The decision came about in a random internet search one day and it wasn't long before they had packed their belongings and moved. She is still emphatic that the house found them. This oceanfront community is located at the eastern tip of Long Island. The town is wonderfully laid-back in feel and home to five thousand acres of beautiful beaches and parkland—perfect locations to suit her classical clientele. It also offered the quiet and privacy Lisa-Marie enjoyed while working, and a welcome respite for her husband when he is looking for time off from his frenetic travelling schedule.

Things became very simple in her professional life. All shoots were now done in Montauk. She purchased a

Steinway Grand Piano for their home that doubled as a prop for shoots with pianists as well as a relaxing distraction for her. Musicians had the choice of arranging their own transportation or having her set up a limo. In the solitude of her own home, they finalize a wardrobe choice, choose the concept, agree on a location, and finish make-up and styling. Then it's off to complete the shoot. Location was now the easiest to decide.

"Being in Montauk, you've got the beach, the forest, the cliffs, and our home we are always changing around. I make the shoot about them. I just make them beautiful." Time-consuming post-production is completed while relaxing in the comfort of her own home. It's a match made in heaven and she is still thankful they made the move. "Our house is the centre of our world. It's my studio, my husband's studio, and now my son's studio. [Sascha picked up the camera professionally starting in his teens.] It's also the gathering place of all our friends. There is never a dull moment here and it's helped us grow all of our careers."

One thing that often happens as she works with musicians is they end up sharing their stories. It helps them relax and distracts them from the camera, which they often don't consider a friend. Each story is personal. To become a professional musician is not easy and there are many sacrifices along the way, much like a professional athlete. Practice and training are the first goals in their day. Family, friends, and having fun take second place. Sport teams and clubs in school are a pipe dream.

Probably the most touching story throughout Lisa-Marie's

photographic career is that of a young violinist with a very famous father—Alec Hou. He was the first person in 1970s China to be permitted to perform Western classical music after the Cultural Revolution had banned it. Her name was Susanne Hou.

"Susanne came to New York to shoot with me and told me her story. Her father had been a concert violinist in China. He was caught practising and had his house boarded up. Eventually he was put in a prison cell for four years with a bucket to use as a toilet, but he finally escaped to Canada with his wife and daughter. When she was four she asked, 'Dad, when are you going to teach me how to play the violin?' He was elated that he could pass on his gift to his daughter, so they marched out and bought her the smallest violin they could find. It was still way too big for her. There was a little maple log in his fireplace. He took it out and hand carved her a nine-inch violin. She played her first note on this instrument and to this day will never forget the sound. 'It wasn't pretty, but it was music to me.' He was her teacher throughout most of her young life and there were many dinners she would miss because she had to get something right before she was allowed to eat. But in the end, she was thankful because she could now do it with her eyes closed."

Now internationally recognized, Hou has gone on to perform all over the world and has received many honours, including the opportunity to perform and work on rare, priceless violins. In 2008, she was offered the chance to choose a precious violin to borrow for a specific time.

A 1735 Guarneri worth six million dollars, once owned by Austrian composer Prince Fritz Kreisler Guarneri, del Gesù, spoke to her. After four years, she regretfully had to let it move on to another worthy musician. For her final performance before she had to return the much-loved instrument, she chose to play Beethoven's Violin Concerto in D major, the very same composition her father performed in China after the end of the Cultural Revolution. Her parents were in attendance.

Such stories as these are the bread and butter of Lisa-Marie's time on set.

In 2010, the Winter Olympics were held in the Mazzuccos' former home town of Vancouver. It was an exciting time. Lancôme Canada approached the couple with an interesting offer that allowed them to again work together while exploring new territory. Their answer was a resounding yes. The project was to create images to be used on limited edition make-up boxes for the company's Olympic Gold Fascination Campaign.

Raphael had been creating mixed media artwork for the last five years—layers of photographs, painting, and resin. They decided as a team to try and bring this concept to the new shoot. Initial photographs were taken of the models and printed. Then the two set to work. The images were altered in an organic process by brushing, dabbing, mashing, and sprinkling on make-up. The altered images were then photographed. What Lancôme Canada ended up with were unique boxes adorned with limited edition artwork and filled with their product. A perfect keepsake.

They were a hit. Even more fun was the chance to return to Vancouver on a promotional trip and reconnect with friends and family.

The normal ebb and flow of every industry means there are times off when bookings come further apart. Now is one of those times. Fewer bookings means more free time. True to form, that means embracing a new focus for all her unbridled energy. This time it came outside the realm of art and launched Lisa-Marie back into the world of sports. There was no toe in the water when approaching this new interest. It was a full cannonball into the deep end. The last three years have been filled with a mass of tennis lessons and constant games. She logs three to four hours a day on the court practising and playing. Add in a couple of out-of-town four- to five-day tennis camps a year and you can see her intense commitment. It's right in character with any new direction she takes.

"You know me. When I do something, I go all the way or I don't bother. One high moment for me last year was winning my singles league."

With over ten plus years as a photographer, Lisa-Marie has accumulated a stunning body of work that is second to none. Her résumé includes over one hundred album covers featuring many top names in the music industry—both in the United States and internationally. While this may be an ebb moment, there are still those wonderful photographic jobs that arise, such as the opportunity to work with the great Itzhak Perlman on both his album cover and promotional shoots. And it's to her credit that the talent she is most known for is her ability to put clients at ease and capture what is exceptional—finding a way to draw out and showcase each artist's strengths, confidence, and unique beauty.

Lisa-Marie never trained for make-up, styling, or photography. She met the challenges by feeling, by embracing the work already there, by learning on set, and by doing it full tilt with all her passion and focus engaged. There are lots of highs—most importantly the birth of her son Sascha—and the lows—not that many and easily forgotten. Her innate energy and curiosity mean there will always be a new interest to embrace.

Success?

"I measure success by how I feel in the morning. If I'm happy, looking forward to the day, pain free, injury free, healthy, my family happy—then I am WAY successful. If I made more money, I would just spend it. If I had less to work with, my house would be smaller and probably not in Montauk. Either way I'd be happy."

Caroline MacGillivray

"I've never wanted anyone to feel small or invisible and that has really shaped who I am and the work I do. It's all about empowerment—what makes people's eyes light up. It's about making people feel good and helping them own their own power."

Every city—and, let's face it, most towns—has one of those areas. It's where the buildings are run down, the streets aren't as clean, graffiti abounds, shopping carts piled high with possessions are part of the regular décor, and "Any spare change?" are the most common words heard. The disenfranchised find a home here. They have nowhere else to go. You see them wandering the streets during the day or huddled in worn sleeping bags at night trying to stay warm. They live in a bubble of poverty, hunger, and violence. We drive through only when absolutely necessary, never showing the area to visitors and avoiding walking these streets at night at all costs. It's every city's private shame.

The people who populate these areas struggle to get through each day. How do they end up living on the street? The answer is not simple as there many paths leading here. It can happen to anyone. There are the unemployed who lost their jobs and were unable to find a new one in time;

teenagers who have run away from impossible homes and foster homes; individuals struggling with difficult mental and physical challenges; women who were recruited into the sex trade when young and naïve; drug addicts, many who developed their habit after experiencing a serious accident; and some unfortunate souls that simply fell through the cracks. The problem is, once living on the streets, it's almost impossible to leave. They no longer have access to a shower, clean clothes, a phone number to give prospective employers, an address to receive mail, or even the ability to use a computer to type and send résumés.

In Vancouver, British Columbia, this area is called the Downtown Eastside (DTES).

Fortunately, charities have stepped in to offer help, with many new ones launched in the last ten years. Founding a charity organization to help the disenfranchised is an act born of true compassion. It has to be a part of a person's DNA. It means long hours, no paycheque until the charity is well-established, constant efforts to get media attention and acquire donations, all while trying to turn the focus to the clients who desperately need your time and energy. Add an outside job to pay your own bills and the enormity of the task is clear. But for those who choose this route, the rewards of creating true change are well worth it. Just ask DTES's "Beauty Night Society" founder Caroline MacGillivray. While early on she envisioned herself being a star on Broadway, there were already signs at a very young age that her heart would lead her to this worthy calling.

The best description of MacGillivray as a child would

probably be complex, like that of a gemstone that offers many different facets. It would start with her ethnic diversity—Scottish on her father's side and fifth-generation Canadian-Chinese on her mother's. Another would be the shy girl seen at school and in front of company, alongside the energetic, exuberant girl seen while doing anything creative, especially musical theatre. Then there were her future dreams. On one hand were her aspirations to become a famous actress and on the other, a plan to help those in need. The last grew from life experience.

"I studied ballet for years. Many of my friends had eating disorders. There were no resources whatsoever. As a kid I envisioned a centre where people who were unemployed, who had an eating disorder, or alcohol and drug problems could come in. I was only nine or ten at the time, so pretty young. There would be access to counsellors right away. There would be recycled clothing available and tailors to reshape the garments. There would be support groups."

This was the first hint of what destiny had in store.

MacGillivray credits both her parents with having a huge influence on her path. Her father, Alex, was a wonderful role model who passed on his love of journalism. He wrote for *The Vancouver Sun* for over forty years—starting as a freelancer in his late teens. By the time he reached retirement, he had risen through the ranks to become the Senior Assistant Managing Editor and was included in the *Sun*'s one-hundred-year commemorative book.

"There's a lot of my dad in me. I used to steal his big old Sony tape recorder and use it to interview my stuffed toys.

I made up all the voices. I think that's why, when I became an actor, I made most of my money doing voice-over work in the studio. I'd been practising for a long time."

For years, every time she auditioned for a role she was known as "Alex's kid." Everyone laughed when, five or six year ago, people started to ask if he was "Caroline's dad."

MacGillivray's mother brought an entirely different influence which began with an intriguing family history. Her great-grandfather had emigrated from Canton to work on the railroad during the time of Canada's head tax, a fixed fee charged to each Chinese person entering Canada in the late 1800s. Great-grandmother also came from Canton—a move that allowed her to escape the painful practice of foot binding. Strong women role models abound in MacGillivray's family, including an aunt who was the first female Chinese stockbroker. Her mother also had a determined nature and multiple talents. From childhood she was a genius with numbers, which led to a daytime career as an accountant. But her performer side would come out at night while dancing in the chorus in the Marco Polo Club's evening show. While her daughter definitely inherited those performing genes and inner determination, she left the math genes behind.

When talking about her childhood, MacGillivray fully admits she could be difficult at times, for many reasons. She was painfully shy at school. Being mixed race opened the door to teasing and when her body started to develop early, fuel was added to the fire. By grade three, she was already wearing a bra and bullying became more frequent.

"I was the geekiest kid and used to get punched. I would come home with bruises. The teachers never did anything. Back then you were told, 'That's what boys do when they like you.' I still remember walking home with my aunt one day and two boys who had failed grade one were following us and spitting. I actually had to put my umbrella up."

Creative pursuits—alone or in the company of other children—brought out a totally different side. Here MacGillivray's deep-seated, fun-loving nature found expression. Producing plays was a passion from early on. Her dad created a stage in the back yard and any willing child would be added in. She spent hours on an exercise rebounder in the basement, singing away while performing toe touch jumps and other crazy stunts. It is no surprise to learn she still finds leaping a joyous activity as an adult. Journalism—another artistic outlet she enjoyed—also began to exert itself.

"I remember going through the Sears catalogs to pick out everything I wanted for Christmas. The first thing I recall getting was a typewriter that I learned to use early on. My mother, always practical, pointed out if I didn't make it as an actor, I could type."

Her mother had a few mandatory goals that didn't always sit well with this big dreamer. The first couple—do well in school and get that all-important high school diploma. It was a hard sell. What did history and math have to do with a life on the stage?

"All through high school I spent a lot of time arguing with my mother. What was the point of going to algebra or chemistry? None of those would pertain to my real life because I was going to be an actor. What I really wanted was to go to that school in the movie *Fame*."

It is only through her mother's sheer determination that MacGillivray earned a high school diploma.

Her mother's next mandatory goal for her daughter was to take ballet. MacGillivray was short, stocky, and curvy at a young age, which meant she didn't have the standard ballet body. Although it took a lot of compromising, in the long run it ended up being fabulous preparation for stage as well as for life.

"The one thing I took away from ballet was persistence. The older I get, the more I see that all that rigorous training and how hard I pushed was good. I think if anyone wants to do something, just dive in, even if it's not the right thing. We always learn skills that can be applied to other areas of our lives."

Acting quickly took over MacGillivray's life and she happily lived and breathed it, day in and day out. There was no point in doing theatre in school as the semi-professional stage had already come calling. Her first break was in Vancouver's Theatre Under the Stars (TUTS) summer schedule.

"I was doing the kids chorus in TUTS by the time I was twelve. I absolutely loved anything to do with musical theatre. My first role was in *Damn Yankees* and I had a one-line solo, but by the first performance, had memorized everyone's lines."

Ironically, the choreographer for this show was Rosanne

Hopkins who had choreographed MacGillivray's mother years earlier at the Marco Polo Club. The budding actress was in awe and devotedly watched Hopkins closely during every rehearsal. Giving their daughter permission to participate in TUTS offered her parents leverage to keep the actor on track in other areas. Adding the much-desired singing and jazz lessons rested solely on keeping grades up in school and staying in ballet.

Singing lessons are the first order of the day for anyone hoping for a career in musical theatre. Learning how to use your voice properly, to create phrasing, and to know when to breathe are important to the quality of a singer's performance. These same skills would prove important years down the road when running her charity.

"You'll laugh. When I first started doing public speaking for Beauty Night, I used to use the same technique. I would go through my speeches and put check marks in so I knew where to breathe. The other thing that is interesting is that Cantonese was my first language. [As a result] if I'm not warmed up, my voice is soft and in my throat."

Outside classes, there was the constant round of auditions to attend. Others might consider auditioning a chore, but for MacGillivray it was exciting. As the movie and television industry was still in its infancy in Vancouver, stage was the only route to stardom. New York City and the bright lights of Broadway were her ultimate goals.

In high school, her busy schedule—singing, dancing, auditioning, performing, and keeping up her school work—occupied a lot of her time, but she still enjoyed crazy times with her friends. She remembers one summer in particular.

"I was fourteen and writing a book called, '101 Ways To Pick Up Boys.' My friends and I would practise at Vancouver's Expo 86. My favourite? If I had a camera I would approach a guy and say, 'Excuse me, can you take a picture with us. Why? Because I think you're cute.'"

Looking back now, she appreciates that this normal flirtatious teenage period of her life was important to learning how to embrace a healthy, adult view of sensuality.

MacGillivray was over the moon when she landed a part in a touring show in grade twelve, something several of her friends were already doing. It would mean hitting the road, completing school online, earning a paycheque, and becoming a true professional in every sense of the word. The answer from her parents was dismaying. "No." She had to finish high school first. Both parents realized that earning a diploma probably would fall by the wayside if they said, "Yes." Upset but resigned, she graduated and began to study acting in earnest.

The actor's twenties were full of fun, friends, and her first love; all centred totally around her passion for musical theatre. Here her natural, friendly nature went a long way toward opening doors. One of her first industry jobs came about through a random bathroom encounter. MacGillivray liked a woman's lipstick, so she opened a conversation. That connection led to being hired by Tourism Vancouver for their *Official Visitor's Guide* where the actor ended up writing freelance articles, doing voice-overs for ads, and recording the many messages on their telephone answering system. This job in turn led to work doing studio voice-overs. In acting, it's all about connections.

MacGillivray decided to further her acting studies at Studio 58, but it wasn't smooth sailing. "It was an amazing program but not the right fit for me." The Gastown Actors Studio came next. She had always wanted to study with Mel Tuck, the school's director and founder. This was her chance. Tuck was producing a musical—*Pack Up Your Troubles*—which she was lucky enough to be a part of.

"He was brilliant. I was intimidated in his class for a very long time. I would get my notes after a scene and it would take me ages to figure out what he meant. I also was exposed to some truly amazing classmates. It was a phenomenal experience."

The actor was enthusiastic and positive by nature so she struggled to connect with emotions like anger and rage. One class in particular pushed her hard to explore those depths. MacGillivray's mother had passed away recently. Despite their previous conflicts, she truly loved and missed her mother. But opening the door to what was going on inside not only ended up creating more emotional depth, but opened the door to healing.

"We were doing the scene from *Steel Magnolias* where Julia Roberts' character tells her mum she is pregnant. All the character wanted was for her mother to be happy for her. As the pregnancy could possibly kill her daughter, her mother is upset. My teacher, Michael David Sims, kept pushing me, 'Come on Caroline, start again.' I was getting more angry and frustrated until I finally burst into ugly, angry tears that streamed down my face. We started the scene again and I was choking and spitting out the words until he called, 'Cut.' I am in a ball crying and shaking and he says, 'I'm in love with your rage. When are you going to stop hiding?' He also told me I was one of the smartest people he had ever met, and if I could stop picking characters to play, I'd have a lot more going on because there was so much more depth to me than I let anyone see. Sometimes I think everyone should go to theatre school. The work they do can be incredibly intense therapy and a journey of self-discovery."

MacGillivray met scores of talented people at this school. One such person was Carina. After graduation, Carina went on to work in a transition home for sex workers who had survived and were trying to change their lives. Touched by these women, she wrote a film script called *Happy Birthday, Julie*, about a fourteen-year-old girl who moves to suburbia, tries really hard to fit in, and then is recruited by her best friend and that friend's boyfriend into the sex trade. MacGillivray was cast in the leading role.

At the time, MacGillivray was extremely frustrated at being typecast by the film industry in the role of a younger, bitchy girl due to her very young looks and bright personality, so the chance to stretch her wings was welcome. The actress ended up not only acting in the film, but helping to co-produce, cast, and deal with all the union requirements. This role ended up changing her life as it led to the founding of Beauty Night Society.

MacGillivray is the first to admit her initial venture into helping in the DTES was not motivated by altruistic concerns. She wanted to do background research so the character she was playing in Carina's play could be as authentic as possible. The Gastown Actors Studio was on the edge of the DTES, so she first started by observing and getting to know the homeless people she passed daily while walking from the bus—watching how people walked, talked, and interacted. If they asked her for change, she answered, "No." Instead, she offered a cup of coffee and a muffin, along with a willingness to listen.

"I heard a lot of amazing stories and really became aware of some of the issues they were dealing with on a daily basis. For example, if they walked in to the coffee shop before me, people were ready to shoo them out. Sometimes the owner would give me a dirty look, but I was a regular customer so he had to tolerate me bringing in somebody who may not be a person they envisioned as their ideal customer."

She had already learned a bit about prejudice from within her own family situation and from other ethnic friends at school, but this world was new to her.

The actor also began to volunteer at an organization called Wish Vancouver Drop-In Centre. She spent volunteer hours working in the kitchen offering food to those who walked through the door in high emotional states. Why? It was the first point of contact for women who had often experienced violence and were dealing with shame at their situation. MacGillivray was touched deeply. Each client became a real person deserving of respect. She treated the people who came in with a warm smile and a ready ear as if they were entering a real restaurant. She embraced them just as they were. In return, these women gave back just as much as they received and showed true courage in facing life.

"I loved hearing their stories. I loved seeing the generosity of some of the women. They are very accepting. I think that's one of the biggest misconceptions about the DTES. There is a lot of violence. We see a lot of the trauma, the homelessness, and the poverty. But what's missing is that the area has such a beautiful heart. These women have been very good to me."

Fourteen years later, it is the generosity of these clients that continues to inspire her.

The idea for Beauty Night first appeared in her childhood. Now, life was leading her full circle back to that early idea. There were two experiences at Wish in particular that provided her with inspiration. MacGillivray shares both stories whenever and wherever she can promote her charity and each time they are told with the same passion. The first story is about when one of the women asked her what it was like to be a kid. The question came out of nowhere.

"I asked her what she meant and she responded, 'When I was four, my father was sleeping with me. By the time I was six, he was selling me. And by the time I was ten, I was in and out of so many foster homes, it was safer on the street.' That shocked me, because I didn't realize this was happening here—in my own city."

As the conversation continued, it came out that the woman also had endometriosis, ovarian cancer, and HIV. This was not the wonderful, sleepy town MacGillivray had envisioned. The two quickly became friends.

The second experience occurred one night when MacGillivray and this woman were at Wish, hanging out. A client who had obviously experienced trauma that day came in. The woman was in really bad shape. She didn't want to eat, didn't want to sleep, didn't want to call the police, and didn't want to fill in a victim services report. What she did want was a shower. Everyone was concerned and tried to approach her, but she ignored them and started going through the donations for clean clothes. Surprisingly, out came a curling iron. MacGillivray noticed that it touched something raw, deep inside the woman.

"After she plugged it in and it got hot, I realized she couldn't raise her arms to do her own hair. She looked like she was ready to cry, so I offered to do it for her."

Laughs followed as the future Broadway wannabe had absolutely no talent at hair styling. Although the offer of a ballet bun was put on the table, in the end the pair decided on French braiding. The client also asked to have her nails done, which was hilarious as MacGillivray had some of the worst nails on the planet so was worried her efforts wouldn't be good enough. But the woman's comment on leaving brought home the importance of these small kindnesses.

"She made a joke after about me making her feel more human—that was huge—and then when she walked out of there, she just looked taller. It reminded me of when I was eighteen and working for a clothing company. I got a kick in my belly when I'd help someone pick an outfit they were happy with and decide to walk out the store wearing it. That's what Beauty Night was like at the beginning."

It took time for Beauty Night to become a reality. MacGillivray loved working with Wish and even served on their board, but in 2000 the demand for services had grown to the point that a separate organization was needed to handle it. Every time she showed up, more and more women were asking for makeovers. At times, it created tension, as she was there to fill the volunteer position she had accepted, but makeovers were what the clients wanted. She tried to balance the expectations of Wish and these client as best she could. A friend who worked for MAC Cosmetics donated product from her kit to bring to the centre each week and fortunately a roommate had taught MacGillivray enough about sanitation to do it safety. However, she was concerned.

"I was really worried I was going to get fired as a volunteer. I had developed all these amazing relationships with the women. I loved volunteering there—Wish is a great organization—but I also recognized what I was doing was not a fit."

After speaking with the board, it became clear it was time to launch a companion organization to fill this need. The list of to-dos was long. MacGillivray couldn't fill the growing demand alone. She had to recruit more people who hopefully had experience in hair, make-up, nails, and any other personal services that could be offered to Beauty Night clients. She needed a space and had many in-depth discussions about security with her volunteers so they could offer a truly safe environment. After three months of conversations and coffee, the approval for the very first Beauty Night came through as well as permission to hold it in the gym at a local church. From that moment forward, she has not turned back.

Beauty Night offers disenfranchised women a chance to step out of their fractured world for an evening. There are already many charities that focus on housing, food, and providing training, but experience showed there were other needs to be met. Change comes in two ways—from the inside out and from the outside in. Sometimes, people doubt the latter, but studies show even the act of putting a smile on our face—no matter what we feel like at the time—has an effect on our sense of wellbeing. On these evenings, the women come in to take part in wellness activities, life-skills development, and makeover services. Why? This simple service offers victims of violence the knowledge that touch can be a positive thing. The sheer act of touching a person in kindness helps with healing.

MacGillivray was honoured to be one of several to receive a 2002 *Flair Magazine* Volunteer Award. It meant a trip to Toronto, a photo shoot, and a lovely reception. The award also brought a great deal of national and international media attention for Beauty Night, which opened the doors to expansion. A young woman in Toronto, Ann Roche, became interested in starting a branch of Beauty

Night in her city. With the increased exposure brought by MacGillivray's award, volunteers and corporate sponsors moved into place over the next few years to offer services not only in Vancouver, but in several new locations. Beauty Night ran evenings in Toronto from 2002 to 2010, in Prince George from 2007 to 2010, and in Victoria from 2003 to 2007. Each location had a core volunteer in place who kept the program on track.

In 2010, the recession hit North America and several long-time volunteers had to step down. The loss of funds and key leadership meant that there wasn't enough support to continue the programs in other cities. When an organization grows as quickly as Beauty Night did, a temporary pause like this offers the perfect opportunity to step back, re-organize, fine tune the business plan, and set realistic goals.

Many things came together. MacGillivray stepped down from being on the charity society's board to focus more time on actively running the charity. Then came a unique opportunity to get professional assistance through a British Columbia Social Venture Partners grant application. Each of the three finalists—Beauty Night was one—was paired with a business professional.

"We were able to get right back to the basics—this is what we needed to do. Now we had a solid foundation and criteria for our growth."

Lastly, MacGillivray attended a course called The Board Chair Academy run by Vantage Point—a company that offers leadership training for those working in the volunteer sector. "It really helped to streamline our organization's focus and values and gave me the leaderships skills I needed to take it to the next level."

Although the demands of running Beauty Night meant MacGillivray's time was at a premium, it was also important for her to find a way to cover her daily living expenses. The answer involved embracing several new directions, each with a focus on bringing wellness to an even wider audience. The first was radio, which was and still is a great match for the former actress. In 2005, childhood friend and sex educator, Julia Saunders was looking for a producer/co-host for Juice Box Radio. MacGillivray was already writing a weekly column on dating and relationships for *Urban Trendz*, so she quickly agreed to join the team.

"It was a learning curve going from print to radio and took a while for me to be comfortable on the air by myself. The show focused on sexual health. When Julia went on maternity leave, I was asked by the station if I had another show [idea], so I pitched 'Sexy in Vancouver'—a 60-minute talk show covering sexual and relationship health."

The underlying philosophy—gaining confidence as well as connecting mind and body—was right in line with her message of wellness. The show was a hit and is now in its tenth season on air at Juice Box Radio.

In 2004, she added pole dancing instructor at Aradia Fitness to her résumé. While this may seem an unusual choice given the sexual violence often experienced by the clients at Beauty Night, it makes perfect sense to MacGillivray. She started to take pole dancing classes reluctantly in order to write an article for a local magazine, but quickly fell in love with the combination of dance movement, embracing one's sensuality, and a great physical work-out. The classes were filled with an amazing group of women who offered a supportive environment and a total lack of judgment—something rarely experienced during those many years of dance classes. It wasn't long before her enthusiasm led to an invitation to become an instructor.

"Have you ever taken a pole dancing class? If not you're missing something. It's so much fun. It's all about what makes their eyes light up. It's about making them feel like women. It's about empowerment."

Next came schooling to become a Medical Qigong practitioner in 2014. Qigong is one of the four branches of Chinese medicine and deals with aligning the physical, emotional, and spiritual energetic fields to achieve health. Exercises and treatments focus on purging stagnant Qi (life force), tonifying, and regulating the energy. While her practice—treatments, classes, workshops, and distance healing—is not limited to the disenfranchised, the bonus of being able to offer another step to wellbeing to Beauty Night clients was an added plus.

"I asked my teachers, Wendy Lang and Minke de Vos, if I might be able to ask some of their students if they wanted to become volunteers for Beauty Night to offer treatments and classes for our participants. Instead they offered me a scholarship to train to become a teacher. I am so grateful."

This same year, MacGillivray spent July attending a month-long Yoga instructor's course. Yoga has been offered at Beauty Night events since 2007, but becoming an instructor allowed her the ability to step in and run classes if needed. It is also one more tool to help her clients connect mind and body.

"Anything that connects people to their body, mind, and spirit is really key as it helps them feel ownership. By doing all the self-care—filling ourselves up, making sure we surround ourselves with good people that nourish us, making sure our cup is full to overflowing—then we have an abundance to share with others."

Beauty Night changes lives—both for the clients and the volunteers. And in return, they show a generosity that truly touches one's heart. Viola (alias) was disabled in a car accident as a teenager and ended up struggling with pain, addiction, and a lack of employment. Now in her fifties and living on disability, she became clean and sober over the last few years while participating in Beauty Night. In gratitude, this client is always giving back. One night this meant offering a few dollars to purchase more emery boards when the volunteers ran out. Another time she carefully arranged handpicked flowers, wrapped them in paper as though she'd bought them in a store, and presented them to MacGillivray in thanks. And then there was the night this client brought her mother. MacGillivray is still touched by the memory.

"That night was her mother's birthday so she brought her along. Toward the end of the night, she asked me how many people were there—twelve at the time—and then said she'd be right back. I thought she went outside to smoke, but she went to McDonalds and bought everyone an ice cream. It was so sweet."

Then there is Joyce (alias). When Beauty Night in Toronto was launched in 2002, MacGillivray was concerned about money as she was paying all costs out of her own limited funds. Joyce was one of Beauty Night's first participants and offered to donate her welfare cheque to help the new venture. When MacGillivray refused the offer, Joyce explained, "If you can make the ladies in Toronto feel the way you made me feel about myself, the money will be well spent." In the end, an agreement was made to accept a two dollar donation.

On the volunteer side, past participant Jennifer Allen was encouraged by MacGillivray to start her own initiative. Inspired, Allen went on to start Jen's Kitchen—an outreach program for Vancouver's sex workers who have left the violent streets and are trying to find a new life. Every Tuesday night a team of volunteers heads out to the streets and alleys of the DTES to hand out sandwiches, snacks, and juice boxes. Many of these street women have challenges that cause them to be banned from local food kitchens, so Allen brings the food to them.

Beauty Night has grown by leaps and bounds over the last fourteen years and is being held several times a week in different locations. Growth is only limited by the need to raise the necessary funds. Both volunteers and participants have experienced profound change. But it has not always been smooth sailing. In 2014, a damning letter to the editor in Vancouver's hip newspaper, *The Georgia Straight*, attacked the focus of this charity, calling it embarrassing.

"Caroline MacGillivray and her volunteer crew ought to give the ladies of the night tips on fellatio to help them pull in more cash at their night jobs. Or why not educate them on the new low-carb diet that might keep these ladies sexy and slim?"

The journey to MacGillivray's launch of Beauty Night was founded on such personal experiences gained while talking and sharing with these women that this letter rocked her to her core. What sustained her during this time was both the women who continued to be uplifted by this unique program and the response written by Mary Wreglesworth, Board Member and long-time volunteer.

"Ms. MacGillivray began (and continues) as a volunteer at Wish and, after working with us a few months, recognized that most of our participants only experienced personal touch as part of an exploitative or abusive process. Acting on the accepted belief that everyone needs some physical nurturing for emotional health, she conceived of Beauty Night and single-handedly courted and enlisted the help of hair stylists, manicurists, masseuses, healing touch therapists, and foot therapists. It is difficult to find words that adequately describe the overwhelming success that Beauty Night has become and how much it means to the women who participate—both as volunteers and recipients. For a few hours one night, several times a year, Vancouver's most disadvantaged women can briefly put aside their problems and enjoy what the rest of us take for granted: a good haircut, some pampering, and, most important, the chance to be carefree and frivolous. The all-too-rare glimpses of excitement and pure joy on women's faces make these evenings unforgettable."

One can only add a resounding amen. What these women want to move them forward should be defined by their own needs. Beauty Night offers that chance we all take for granted: to be clean, to be touched in a positive way, to be treated kindly, and to change how we feel about ourselves. Sometimes this needs to happen from the outside in. Yes, housing and food are important, but this charity was created as a supplement to existing programs—not to replace them.

MacGillivray continues to dream big.

"Beauty Night continues to grow at warp speed. The biggest goal is sustainability. Currently we are serving over three hundred women and men each week during our four nights of programming. On a budget of $45,000, we are a one-person staffed show." What is needed is money to hire more staff to better lead the team of volunteers, to increase the wellness and life-skills-development programs, and to meet the growing demand for services. Currently there are twenty-seven charity organizations on the wait list.

How does this dynamo who is juggling so many careers define success? It comes down to living whatever is one's life purpose.

"My mission is to connect people who have disconnected from their bodies. To reconnect them so they feel whole and are able to have healthy relationships and so they can embrace their life's purpose. By choosing to embrace your mission, and let it lead you where it may, life becomes a daring and, dare I say, an exciting adventure!"

William Orlowski

*"How do you define success? There is no secret.
Just do and be brave."*

Tap dance has experienced many changes through the years, evolving as each generation offers its own interpretation. History places tap dance's roots as far back as the mid-1800s with touring minstrel shows. Since that time it has found an ever-expanding home in vaudeville reviews, on stage in musicals, in dance company tours, in movies, and on television. It shares a kinship with Irish Step Dancing and English Clog Dancing. The sheer energy expressed in performance has made it a popular class amongst young students at dance schools. On stage, it is an art form like no other.

Each tap dancer is like a fine wine—defined by the era they were a part of. The performer is a percussive instrument working in tandem with the music—or even sometimes as the sole sound—and what they bring is a sum total of who they are as artists. Canadian tap icon William Orlowski is no exception. He is classically trained in a way that is out of fashion today. In his routines, there is no heavy stomping to create sound. Less is more. He can create a clear, small tone with the slightest flick of his foot that will carry all the way to the very back row of a theatre, because he understands exactly how the sound should be produced. Dancer, choreographer, teacher, humanitarian. What began as a single class turned into a passion that opened doors to a rich life extending well beyond the dance studio.

Orlowski was born in Brampton, Ontario, in 1952. He admits to being a difficult child.

"I was a brat to my parents and very withdrawn in school—I didn't like it. I lost a sister when I was six and had a hard time that first year. My mother would take me to school and I would go running back home and hide in the closet. Then the teacher would call. I was always making up stories. I think that helped formulate my creative juices."

His family struggled financially, but he somehow managed to go to the matinee at the local movie theatre most weekends. This was the golden age of cinematic musicals. While he watched them all, it was the movies featuring tap dancers that captured his passion. Saturdays afternoons were spent with eyes glued to the silver screen while Fred Astaire, the Nicholas Brothers, Bill "Bojangles" Robinson, and others tapped their way into his heart.

Every week Orlowski would return home and beg his mother for tap dance lessons. She was sure it was just a fad. Add that to the fact money was also an issue, and it's easy to understand why she usually just responded, "Yeah, yeah." This continued week after week until, by age ten, he wore her down. She agreed to pay for half a term, "Just in case you don't like it and want to quit."

His first teacher was Marise White. She and her brother Bobs had been a Vaudeville tap duo called the Allerston

Kiddies many years earlier. When her brother died unexpectedly in a car accident, Marise refused to perform anymore, left the stage, and opened the Marise White School of Dance in Port Credit. It was here that what started as a passion and dream began the slow journey to reality.

That first half term extended into a full year as Orlowski proved to his parents this was more than a passing fad. "I was just in love with tap and couldn't stop. My dad bought me a piece of plywood to use as a floor and I would practise before breakfast and after school. My mother had to haul me out of the basement just to go to bed. I couldn't believe the magic."

At the end of the year, the young, enthusiastic tapper was ready to hit the stage for his first recital, but fate stepped in. White was married to the general manager of a dance hall in Toronto called the Palace Pier, which she used for all recitals. Unfortunately, the hall burned down the night before Orlowski was to perform, so his teacher had to cancel that year's show. However, recognizing his commitment and talent, White insisted wider training was important. Classes in ballet and jazz with dancer/choreographer Gladys Forrester were added to his schedule.

Choosing dance as a focus in the 1960s was a brave decision for any boy, one that could only be motivated by passion. The choice came with serious repercussions. Bullying was a daily occurrence. Orlowski was teased constantly, physically beaten up, pushed up against brick walls, punched, and called every name in the book. What carried him through was sheer stubbornness and the fact that he truly believed in what he was doing. In time the humour of some of those early experiences rose to the surface.

"One of the boys was particularly cruel to me. Every day he would try to pin me up against the brick wall and beat me up, but I learned to divert his attention. I would say, 'Have you seen this trick I can do—the splits?" He would say, 'No,' so I would do it for him. Then the next day I would try it again and he'd say, 'I've seen that already. What else have you got?' I'd have to come up with something new every day."

Orlowski credits his classical dance training with providing a deeper understanding of music and how the rhythm of tap becomes a part of the performance—something often sadly missing in the studio today. Now training is often less defined and anything goes. A piano in the studio offered live music and the pianist taught him how to read and feel eighth notes, quarter notes, rests, and the technique of which muscles he was using to perform each dance step. The lack of this knowledge limits what a dancer can bring to the stage no matter how talented they are.

"A shuffle can have any rhythm. It can be dotted eighths or sixteenth notes. It could be straight eighths or thirty-second notes, and it all comes from different areas of the legs. How can you expect to do a proper 'wing' when you don't know what it is? It should be very graceful and very delicate. I just scream in horror at people snapping their knees and rolling over the wrong side of their ankle to do wings."

This early training paid off. Later on in his career,

Orlowski would perform a difficult piece where he had to complete thirty-two demanding battement wings in sequence. He completed them with such subtlety that a tap mentor reviewing the performance mentioned there could have been more. More? This sequence was almost impossible to dance as choreographed.

After high school, Orlowski moved to the bright lights of Toronto. He was only seventeen at the time. By age eighteen, he had scored an audition and landed a part in Ann Murray's first television special with Glen Campbell. From then on, the jobs started to roll in. There were tons of commercials including ones for Orange Crush and Pepsi, as well as numerous shows for television. He continued training, now with top names in Canadian tap—icons who went on to become mentors—such as Paul Draper, Jack Lemen (not the actor), Bob Van Norman, and Alan and Blanche Lund. The memories of this time are still strong.

"Those were the last days of variety television and I got hooked into it. There were a group of us that were constantly employed by people producing special shows or musicals. I'm glad I had that experience because it taught me a lot about choreography, watching, listening, paying attention, and learning. That's what most kids don't do now. They talk, yap, and don't listen—they just do it, whatever it is."

Sometimes things ran smoothly with few retakes. Other times, it was a long process. And unfortunately, sometimes things went horribly wrong. There was one Pepsi commercial in particular Orlowski would love to forget. The dancers were in full costume, working hard under the hot lights. They were dancing, going up and down escalators, and the pop bottles were being shaken in the process. In the midst of it all, he dropped his bottle, which exploded on impact. "I'm a butter fingers as anyone will tell you and I dropped the damn bottle. There was disgusting Cola flying everywhere. I was so embarrassed. It got all over everybody's costumes and unfortunately cost them a lot of money."

For eight years, Orlowski worked on stage and in television. Then in 1977, he made a life-changing decision to walk away from it all. It was time for a new direction that would cement his standing as one of Canada's tap icons in his own right and take this dance form from its common role as entertainment into the realm of art. This was the year he chose to become a concert performer, opened the Hoofers Club—one of the first dance schools in Canada devoted specifically to tap—and founded the National Tap Dance Company of Canada with business partner Steve Dymond.

It was a brave decision, but the timing was right. The studio was designed to be a feeder for the tap company. The first week nobody came, but by the third week classes were jam-packed.

"It was the luck of the draw. I had some writers in my class who wrote articles on the school for the *Toronto Star* and *The Globe and Mail*. I was the Sunshine Boy—something the newspaper used theatre people for. It was lucky timing that I had all these people around me who were young and ambitious."

There are so many great stories from this time, but when asked to pick just one, he decided on the story of Nora McLellan, a British Columbia actress, singer, and performer. She walked into the Hoofers Club early on to attend one of the classes. Orlowski was still very new, or as he describes it, "green." He was so into tap that he really had no idea who this person was. The West Coast was a long way away. Some dancers like to loosen the screws that attach the metal taps to their shoes to get an extra jingle out of them—something totally verboten [forbidden] in these classes. The rest is history.

"Nora walked into class to study with me and I didn't know who she was. I heard the noise and loudly said, 'Who's wearing those jingle taps?' She said, 'It's me.' I told her she had to take her shoes off or I would not allow her to stay. She got back at me later at the Shaw Festival. We were doing *Mr. Cinders* with tap shoes and she jokingly said, 'I hear something jingly in the class.' I responded, 'You wouldn't dare!'"

Orlowski did not want to go back to musical theatre and was determined to make a go of it. Great press helped fill classes, but it was important to launch the dance company quickly as well. The studio opened in January 1977 and the company's premiere hit the stage in December that same year. His heart's desire was to build on what he had learned from icons who had been in the industry a long time, honouring his training while bringing something new to the stage. This was art.

"I wanted to be adventuresome. I studied with the

old-timers, but they didn't really speak my language. A lot of people cried when they saw the old-timers, because they said it was so beautiful. I cried but for different reasons. These are the same vaudeville acts they'd been doing for fifty years."

It was time for creation. Time to bring all that this artist had learned to the table and meld it with new ideas to inspire and excite. The answer? Bach's Brandenburg Concerto No. 3. This choreographic work would set the world of tap on fire.

Two week before the company's first performance, Orlowski's father passed away. Orlowski was an emotional wreck. Some felt he should cancel the performance, but that didn't feel right. Out of the ashes of grief came the choreography that was danced in tribute to his father's passing. It was a way to deal with his sorrow that ended up becoming a signature piece.

"There were only six chairs on stage. The music is baroque with a very strict tempo. The dancers started and finished on the floor grovelling with grief while I started on chairs. Near the end they were all flying through the air with balletic Jetés and splits, then landing with cramp rolls—things they weren't used to that I just wanted to try. It was my grief and the one piece that has always stuck."

The critics went wild. It was tap choreography with substance—it was art. One media outlet stated, "Tap triumphed here, emerging as a versatile and legitimate art form."

The company went on to create over fifty original works

that set new boundaries, including *Oliver Button Is a Sissy*, *The Tin Soldier*, *The Hounds of the Baskervilles*, and a choreographic collaboration titled *Feats of Feet*. There was a medley of Gershwin pieces where the part of the drummer in the orchestra was removed and filled in by the rhythm on stage. Another work paired the sound of machine gun fire with the recitation of World War One poetry. The company's originality took the audience by surprise as it was a completely new experience, but for Orlowski the unique ideas just came naturally. Tap was an art form he had loved and embraced since the age of five. To take it to new levels was a joy.

"I would combine ballet and modern technique with tap dancing and put a story behind it. The audience would see a battement and yet hear all these taps come out of the other foot. I could be comical or serious. We have to start looking at substantial works that make a point, that have emotions."

The National Tap Dance Company's innovative mix of choreography including poetry, dance, and live percussion, and serious subject matter made them a must-see for anyone interested in the arts. They began to tour—always with a live orchestra—in Canada, the United States, and throughout Europe and Asia. Performances were to the accompaniment of over twenty live orchestras, including the National Symphony Orchestra, the Hong Kong Philharmonic Orchestra, and L'Orchestre symphonique de Quebec. Notable venues include the John F. Kennedy Center for the Performing Arts in Washington, the Lincoln

Centre in New York City, and the National Arts Centre in Ottawa.

Two trips stand out from this time. The first was to China. The head of Cultural Exchange in Ottawa offered a list of potential visitors to the Chinese Government that included Maureen Forrester, Tommy Hunter, and others. China chose to invite the National Tap Dance Company, because they were the only ones who had never visited before.

It proved to be an exciting adventure. This was pre-Tiananmen Square and the country was still very rustic. The company travelled from city to city, doing eight performances overall. At one venue, the dancers went out for a walk to explore the local town. A group of men were gathered on a street corner looking at a newspaper showing a promotional picture of the tour, reading the review, and talking. With no common language, the performers managed to let these men understand who they were. Lots of smiles and enthusiastic handshaking ensued. While the political climate may not have been ideal, the warmth of the people they met was unquestionable.

Orlowski remembers, "Mao was still around. It was not a very kind place to be, but they were very kind to us. The most fascinating thing was we shared the stage with Chinese performers. In my review of the trip, I wrote that no one really spoke to each other, but volumes were danced."

Another highlight was being invited to perform at the renowned Festival of 2 Worlds in Spoleto, Italy. This prestigious event was founded in 1958 by composer Gian Carlo Menotti and has grown to feature a wide selection of performances—concerts, opera, dance, drama, and visual arts. The name originally referred to North American and European cultures coming together to share the artistic stage. The National Tap Dance Company flew into Rome and then was bused to the small town of Spoleto. It was early fall. The scenery was gorgeous, the food incredible, and the people were, in Orlowski's own words, "Glorious!" For their performance, they chose the company's signature piece—Brandenburg Concerto No. 3. It brought the house down.

Orlowski is an artist who is always driven to change, grow, and embrace new experiences. In 1987, after many years' absence, he felt called to return to the stage. There was the chance to work with director Brian Macdonald on a production of *Dames at Sea*. Orlowski earned his first Dora Mavor Moore Award for Best Choreography. A second Dora Mavor Moore Award followed for *That Scatterbrain Booky*. In addition to his work on stage, there were opportunities in films—he was assistant choreographer for Paramount Pictures' feature film *Stepping Out* starring Liza Minnelli—as well as television credits for both choreography and dancing in shows such as *The Palace Presents*, *Dance Makes Waves*, and *All That Bach*. In 1990, he founded the William Orlowski Tap Dance Projects specifically to create original and innovative choreography.

The Shaw Festival—held at Niagara-on-the-Lake, Ontario—holds a special place in Orlowski's heart. He has won critical acclaim over the years for his work at this festival both as a choreographer and performer, and some of his most memorable experiences are from the time spent here. One director he particularly enjoyed working with was Christopher Newton. There was a graciousness and trust given that allowed the choreographer the freedom to feel out the best way to work with the actors. Many were not dancers and most were intimidated by what might be expected of them. The actors wanted to be told where to put their arms and how to move.

"I asked Christopher for a favour other directors would not give me—to just watch for two days to see who moved what way, who the characters were, and what he was aiming for. I read the director's notes, made my own notes, and observed the way the actors moved as their character, taking note of Christopher's directions to the actors. They tried to be dancers and I said, 'Don't. Just move in character.' Moving across the stage in character was dancing as far as I was concerned. I also told them to allow the same amount of time they spent developing their character to developing that character's movement. The creative process takes six to eight weeks. They understood."

Orlowski is known for innovative choreography, but another of his true gifts is an ability to evaluate a dancer's (or actor's) innate abilities and work with them instead of trying to force them into a set mould that doesn't easily fit. Early in his career, he learned that every dancer is unique in their talents and brings a different sense of timing to the choreography. It is better to work with the actor's natural strengths. For each new work, Orlowski would be brought into the rehearsal space, introduced to the performers, then start by just fooling around to see how they moved naturally. The rehearsal period was used to develop the dance and help the actors be true to their part.

Good choreography allows a dancer's unique character to shine through. Their performance should also be strongly connected to the music, especially when the music is live. It was a lesson brought home in the early days when Orlowski was offered the opportunity to observe Rudolph Nureyev during rehearsal. The ballet great was a guest performer in *Sleeping Beauty* at the National Ballet in Toronto. The conductor was just looking down at his musical score during rehearsals and not observing what was happening on stage—an unforgiveable faux pas to the star performer. Nureyev became red-faced and obviously upset. He was jumping higher and higher, holding poses for longer and longer, trying to get the conductor's attention. Finally, he stopped dancing and said, "Stop, stop, you asshole. You, you watch me!"

Slowly and subtly, a new development entered the picture that would profoundly affect Orlowski's life. It all began way back during his first year performing and choreographing at the Shaw Festival. He was taking a walk with his dogs one day when his head suddenly snapped to the left side. What the heck was going on? His regular doctor had no idea.

Over a five-year period, the random movements continued, and his concern and discomfort increased. There was an early diagnosis of Parkinson's disease that proved to be wrong. Finally, he was sent to a doctor at Mount Sinai Hospital in Toronto where the mystery became clear. After explaining for only twenty minutes what had been happening to his body, she gave him the surprising answer—generalized dystonia, the most severe form. The doctor had seen it before and knew exactly what she was looking at. But what was it?

Today, we would be handed tons of printed material and head back home to do further research on the internet. Back then, there wasn't a lot of information out there and getting to it was much more difficult. No support groups had been formed to share ideas and experiences.

"When I was first diagnosed in 1999, the internet was relatively new so I couldn't access the information I wanted. All I knew was what my neurologist told me, which was that it was a movement disorder."

He headed back to the festival, posted a small notice telling the cast as much as possible and then went back to work with few answers. The disorder was physically very painful to deal with and the lack of connection to other dystonia patients made the journey lonely.

For the next seven years, the symptoms continued to worsen. Work became more difficult. Dystonia involves involuntary, extremely painful, prolonged, and fatiguing muscle contractions, spasms, and tremors, resulting in abnormal body posture. Slowly but surely, his life grew smaller as first his ability to perform and then his ability to endure long choreography sessions lessened. Finally, the day came when he needed a cane to help with walking and, in the end, the dreaded wheelchair. What helped him through this time was sheer stubbornness and an inability to give up.

Research continued. The possibility of a better future was presented the day he qualified for deep brain stimulation—a procedure first tried on Parkinson's patients with encouraging results. It involves a neurosurgical operation in which a brain pacemaker is implanted. As with all cutting-edge medical procedures, there were a lot of psychological and physical tests to make sure he was a good candidate. The answer was yes.

By the day of the surgery, Orlowski's body was so bent and twisted with the muscle contractions he could hardly get out of bed or walk across a room. And he was terrified. This was brain surgery with its inherent risks. You have to be awake for the whole nine-hour operation, which can be frightening on its own. And there is no way to distract yourself from what is happening.

"You can't move, because the surgery is so delicate. So they screw a headgear on that weighs a ton and then they screw you onto the metal edge of the operating table—like Frankenstein. You have to stay alert the whole time, because they ask you questions so they know where they're going. If my speech was off, they adjusted a little knob, and my speech got better. It's weird—like the bionic man being put through the hoops."

A week of hospital recovery followed. Then an IPG (Implanted Impulse Generator) was placed under the skin to control the device.

What happened next was a miracle. "When they turned it on I initially felt a jolt like electricity. The first thing I did was say I had to go to the loo. I stood up and walked by myself. My sister said, 'Look at you.' I didn't even realize what I was doing. I said, 'Oh, my God! You're right!' That was the first inkling that it would work."

It took another week in the hospital for all the muscles to finally relax and then it was back to work. Orlowski was soon back on stage. The first two performances were when he came to the Vancouver International Tap Dance Festival to receive a lifetime achievement award only a couple of months later. However, being a perfectionist, he struggled with the new limitations.

"It felt good to be dancing again, but it was also frustrating. People kept saying I was great, but for me I wasn't. I knew what I used to be able to do versus what I could do now."

Next he was invited to Bamfield by the Sea to compose and perform three new works. It was again that mix of exhilaration and frustration. It took time to embrace reality, but embrace it he did.

"I have come to terms with the fact I can't articulate the sounds as well as I could before, nor do I try."

New opportunities opened up. One in particular proved to be a challenge that used all of Orlowski's talents. A teacher at the Brantford School for the Blind in Ontario took one of his tap workshops and approached him with an idea. Would he like to come and teach rhythms? Orlowski went through a huge learning curve as he tried to figure out how to teach these students. Most had been blind from birth and didn't really have a sense of their body or how to control it. He had to become acutely aware of their spatial habitat and find non-visual ways to get ideas across. In the end, he managed to find unusual solutions.

"I didn't know what I was doing, but was excited to try. If I wanted them to do the shuffle, I would just have them move their toe forward and back. You couldn't get too technical. Sometimes, I would have them put their hands on my leg or foot to feel what I was doing. It was hard work, but I really enjoyed it and fell in love with all the students. There were special moments when they finally clued in and said, 'Oh, I SEE it!' I would respond, 'Yes, you do!' I spent almost a year with those kids and it was really quite special."

This experience, Orlowski's continuing journey with dystonia, and a challenging life have all contributed both to his work and to the way he reaches out to those with disabilities.

"My life has been rather dramatic. Most people don't know that. But I've been through a lot of drama in the best way. It helped my creativity—even my brain surgery—to use my brain cells in a different way. I have empathy with those that deal with a disability. Although I usually have to work with them as a group, I try to find a way to get to them one-on-one—just talk to them. I once had a philosophical discussion with an autistic boy and it was great. He opened up to me, because I listened to him."

One community organization that has benefitted from

the artist's talent is Smile Theatre—a registered charity that brings professional theatre to hospitals and nursing homes throughout Ontario. The organization reaches out to seniors often isolated from cultural experiences.

Art Meets Havoc—which opened in April 2014—was written, directed, and choreographed by Orlowski. It is a two-actor play looking at the process of aging, and based on the life of two real people who were born and died in the same year. The subject is one that is very relevant to Smile Theatre's audiences. The male character is Art Linkletter who was left on the doorsteps of a local preacher and grew up as a preacher's son. The female role is June Havoc—baby June in *Gypsy*—who peaked at age five as a child star. The play shines a light on what they encountered and endured during their life journeys and how they dealt with aging. One managed it successfully, the other unsuccessfully.

Time marches on. As anyone who battles a disabling movement disorder can tell you, there is no going backwards, only periods of stasis followed by new challenges. For Orlowski, this has been particularly true. Each brain pacemaker normally has a life expectancy of four to five years. A new one then has to be implanted. But for Orlowski, the progression of his disorder meant more frequent surgeries. In 2014, he received his fourth device since the initial operation in 2006. Every time, the procedure involves going back into the operating room for another grueling nine-hour surgery, and recovery is always a slow process. Doctors switch most devices to stimulate one side of the brain or the other to suit individual requirements.

Orlowski's new device stimulates both sides at once and he can personally adjust the parameters to what works best for him, without having to go into the doctor's office.

The National Tap Dance Company of Canada, which Orlowski founded, went on hiatus in the late 1990s as a touring company, but continued as a non-profit society running classes and offering outreach programs. Orlowski is the Artistic Director—a position he has embraced for over thirty-five years—and continues to be involved with choreography. One of the latest pieces is an original work being performed in schools called *Able dis Able*. The subject matter addresses the issues of students with disabilities, teaching through movement, dance, and mime. How do we look at them and what obligation do we have to create positive change?

Currently, the company is facing a dilemma typical of all art foundations—money. One area that Orlowski is putting his full weight behind is fundraising to preserve its heritage.

"The company has a repertoire of over fifty original choreographic works—by myself, Paul Draper, and other artists who have worked with us—that we are licensing to protect. We need grants to digitize everything—thirty years' worth of materials. About a year to a year and a half down the road, the choreography will be available for other dancers to try."

Once everything has been documented, catalogued, archived, and recordings transferred to a modern medium, a library is needed to make them available for licensing by other dance companies. New performances could then be staged—just like with classical ballet choreographies. But there is one last catch. Workshops are needed, because no one can perform the work without having technical training first.

Dystonia continues to affect his life, but Orlowski will never stop moving forward. He has to keep busy no matter what the outlet. Painting has proven a creative pleasure that he indulges in often. Oriental watercolours have taken centre stage. Choreography is still a joy, but it has become harder and harder to work the way the industry requires. Usually one is expected to show up for a given number of days and work long, grueling hours until the piece is finished. That is no longer possible.

"I can't choreograph full days now. Fortunately, there are people who will allow me to do half days with intensive work as it's good for me."

Then there is a book he is co-writing with a friend to be called "The History of Tap Dance in Canada." This is a long-term project, but one that is dear to his heart.

"Most [hoofers] are either dying or dead and gone now. We have spent so much time and effort singing the praise of so many in the United States that we have forgotten our own artists. We have neglected our own culture. We have had many great tap dancers here in Canada and we're multicultural, so we've been more accepting."

Orlowski is keenly aware that his style of tap is out of fashion, but still expresses concern that dancers today recognize and demand the technical training and freedom to explore they need to bring something significant to the table. It's not about just stomping to create noise. A tap dancer truly is a rhythm instrument that should be intricately connected to the performance music—the reason Orlowski avoids drums and vocals in his musical selections as they tend to compete instead of blend. He is also concerned that students don't get stuck trying to emulate previous artists instead of exploring new ways of expression.

"You have to pick up the pieces from the past and then step forward with that knowledge. No one seems to be brave enough to do it. There is an unwritten law in tap dancing, 'Though shalt not copy another dancer's steps exactly.' Right now we're being told we must pass on our heritage and history, but there is such an emphasis on the exactness of doing that. They are defying the basic principles the old-timers stood by. They had to make up the steps and be something different from the other dancers. Nostalgia won't survive. Sooner or later there will be a new talent who comes along and pulls us out of this past we're stuck in."

Passion, a love of learning, compassion for the disabled, sheer stubbornness when facing adversity, a well of creativity, and ideas that never stop—these all define William Orlowski. Despite the challenges life has thrown his way, he has become an icon and mentor in his own right. And he embraces every aspect of this journey. Grief, anger, enlightenment, what all human beings are born with— are all sources he has mined to create new and innovative works.

Young tappers are advised to do the same.

In the end he has no script to follow or suggestions to give. His greatest advice is utterly simple and easy to follow, "Just do and be brave."

Julie Salisbury

"What I really want is to help people step into what they're meant to do. To encourage people to really look at their life story and pick up the clues."

Publishing is on the verge of tremendous change, all thanks to the internet and social media. The transition to a whole new way of doing business is still in process, with traditional newspapers, magazines, and book publishers struggling to figure out what direction to take to reap the financial benefits. It is an ever-changing market. What will the industry become in the next five to ten years? One thing is certain. The opportunity for unknown writers to have their voices heard increases on a daily basis.

This is particularly true when it comes to books. Self-publishing was the first door to open for these budding authors. The benefit of self-publishing is obvious. It's all in your hands from start to finish. The negative is the same—it's all in your hands from start to finish. You have full discretion in terms of editing and cover art, but have to pay for quality feedback and do not get access to media channels or book distributors. The cost of outside editing and artwork alone can be daunting. The newest option—hybrid publishers—offers a set-price contract to bring your manuscript to publication. You retain rights, have controlled costs, professional feedback, and access to their industry connections.

Influence Publishing founder Julie Salisbury came into the industry by accident. After self-publishing her own book, she started teaching others how to bring their stories to print. There was no childhood dream of one day owning a publishing house. It was fate leading the way over many years. Accepting the challenge has changed her life. This is not just a job. This company is what defines her. It is what she is meant to accomplish. It is a passion that cannot be denied. The authors she works with become her family in an Ujamaa (cooperative economics) relationship where everyone builds together to create success. Influence Publishing is leading the way in creating a new model for how publishers and writers work together in a way that benefits everyone involved, a model that will hopefully go on to define the industry for years to come.

The path walked before founding this company is not easy to follow at first glance, but each step was an important one. It's only in looking back that the pieces begin to fall into place. There was a very specific before-and-after moment when everything changed, when an inner door opened to a passion long held dormant. Before that moment was an unfocused journey of meeting expectations. The future publisher had to let go of everything she had been taught to embrace in order for her destiny to unfold. And the transition didn't happen overnight. Between the past and this exciting new future there were seven years spent drifting and living a nomadic life sailing the world.

It all began in the Margaret Thatcher years.

Salisbury was born in England. Growing up, she was an awkward kid who struggled to fit in. Her mum loved to dress her and her sister—only fifteen months younger—as twins in outdated fashions with ribbons in their long hair. Everyone else sported more fashionable clothes and wore their hair in very modern page cuts. Needless to say, she spent a lot of time alone. Fortunately, there were books.

"I didn't really have any interests back then. I had no idea who I was. The only thing that caught my attention was English Literature. It was the only subject I excelled at in school. I particularly remember being obsessed with the book, *Equus* by Peter Shaffer—a very dark story about a boy obsessed with horses I studied for my O-Level [graduation] exam." Outside literature, school work was a challenge that she met with sheer hard work.

The next difficulty that set her apart from her peers arose in her teens. She had scoliosis. Treatment for curvature of the spine in those years was pretty medieval. They put you in the hospital, broke your back, inserted a metal rod, and then wrapped you up in a full body cast for six months. Only seventeen at the time, Salisbury was determined to not let the surgery hold her back. Three months were spent in the hospital. Then another three months at home. A tutor helped the determined teenager keep all school work up to date as she did not want to fall behind. School work also helped keep boredom at bay.

"I was never a person who excelled. So, because I was missing so much school, I had to work really hard to keep up. What I discovered a couple of years ago was that I was dyslexic. That went a long way to helping me understand why I excelled in literature and yet struggled in language classes."

After the six months, the full body cast was changed for a smaller one that went from hips to shoulders. It could be worn under clothes several sizes too big, but made her look like she had power shoulders. The smaller cast allowed her to move more freely. Now enrolled in a two-year technical course in business/marketing, she began to walk to school each day with her friends. Getting back into a regular routine was still challenging, but she didn't let the body cast keep her from having a good time.

"I didn't have a lot of friends because I looked like the Honey Monster [a lumbering, loveable cereal mascot]. I had a plaster cast that came right up to my shoulders. When I sat down, it would come up around my ears. But I actually went to night clubs and people asked me to dance. I guess I just looked unusual—a flat chested woman with very large shoulders. A lot of people didn't realize I had a cast on because I wore a square Twenties-style flapper dress. It did hurt a lot to dance, but I just adapted."

There were unexpected logistic challenges that arose daily. One still stands out. Salisbury had decided to walk into town. Determined to be fashionable, she was sporting a pair of very high heels—not easy in a body cast. Then, the unthinkable happened. While crossing a street, one heel became stuck in the pavement—wedged in a gap between the slabs. Jammed tight. The cast meant she wasn't able to bend down to take her shoe off. Not only was it not a safe place to be, it was incredibly embarrassing.

"I'm basically trapped in the middle of the busy street. While I am standing there trying discreetly to not look stupid and trapped in the pavement, one of my teachers walks right by me without stopping. Then he does a double take and comes back. He says, 'Salisbury, are you okay?'" Her answer was a resounding no. Thankfully, he proceeded to dislodge the heel and her journey continued.

Salisbury found her niche in business marketing. Not only did she pass her exams, she excelled despite missing six months of course work during the delivery time. At graduation, she was the overall regional winner of the Business and Technical Education Council's Duke of Edinburgh's Award for outstanding achievement. This meant the nineteen-year-old and her family were invited to Buckingham Palace to receive the honour from Prince Philip in person. The cast was forgotten in the pageantry of the moment, especially when the prince personally shook her hand.

Almost every young English girl dreams of growing up to work at the retailing chain of Marks and Spencer. It's an industry icon in Britain. Salisbury was no exception. Because of the award for excellence, she was selected to be interviewed by the company for their management program. "Excited" didn't begin to describe her emotions. The first stop was to Marks and Spencer to buy her a proper suit to wear to the interview—an amazing experience for the teenager. Unfortunately, because the outfit had to be purchased two sizes too big to fit over Salisbury's body cast, she could never wear it again. The suit also made her look a bit odd as her body cast seriously accentuated her shoulders. The only memory of this special suit is a quick snapshot taken just before her journey to Marks and Spencer began.

High hopes to be hired were quickly dashed when the interview did not go as expected. There was a class system in Britain in those days that opened doors for the privileged who attended private schools (called "public" schools in England) and held back those without those important credentials. This was Salisbury's first experience where this system affected her personally.

"I went into the interview and had a panel in front of me. They asked the most ridiculous questions. The stupidest one? 'Do you feel disadvantaged because you didn't go to public school?' Another. 'Do you feel disadvantaged because you're a girl?' The answer was no. It was my wake-up call for how much the class system existed in England. It's everything in terms of work, and your success is judged on what you look like, what your class is, what your accent is like. As far as I'm concerned, it's still the same today, just more subtle. So I didn't get the job, but by then I didn't want the job."

Salisbury was quickly hired by an industry that ignored the old boys' network and respected her drive and innate talents. In the end, the position that proved most interesting was Product Development, It was here that she soared. This industry experience would be invaluable years later when building her own company—Influence Publishing—and developing a "product" she grew to love, her authors. Although surrounded by co-workers, close relationships continued to prove illusive. Those she counted as friends were few and far between.

"I enjoyed going to work with suppliers, visiting garment factories, but I was still very reserved. I was always the one sitting at the desk in the corner by myself. When I went to the canteen at lunch time, I was always the one sitting alone. I was a very, very different person when I was in England."

While Product Development proved a good match for Salisbury's talents, boredom would always be a problem as the work became more routine. Fortunately the head hunters came calling. Between the ages of eighteen and thirty-two, she was off to a new job about every eighteen months. Each one offered a promotion and a higher salary—sometimes double the previous one. The new challenge would be enough to carry her interest for a while, then she would hit the wall again and accept a new position. By thirty-two she owned a Mercedes, was flying around the world first class, had just married her partner of several years, and was enjoying all the perks that came with status. Her parents were very proud.

But something was missing.

The Margaret Thatcher years had a huge influence on every man, woman, and child living in Britain. Thatcher's mantra was, "There are no free gifts in this life. If you work really hard, you can claw your way up to the next class." It was all about materialism and money. Each step of Salisbury's journey up to this moment was like ticking something off a checklist that was supposed to make her happy—job, house, husband, Mercedes, three cats (Parsley, Sage, and Thyme), RRSP, pension. Activities—sometimes crazy ones—would be embraced to fill the empty moments. These were always a challenge, as that early treatment for scoliosis meant she lived in daily pain. No matter. She would rather have fun and live with the pain than sit at home in a state of boredom.

A position opened up in a company called Fine Arts Developments when Salisbury was in her thirties. The new job required constant travel to the Far East for up to three weeks at a time—the Philippines, Bangkok, Thailand, and Taiwan. Some might consider it fun, but for Salisbury it became a chore and a wake-up call.

"The last trip I was on was to the Philippines. I flew first class, arrived at night, and took a taxi to this luxury hotel. When I woke up in the morning I felt disoriented, so I went to the big glass window and opened the curtains. Outside was a slum with kids running around in bare feet. I remember thinking how can this be? I am cocooned in this safe, luxurious world, and right outside the window—right in front of me—is poverty."

Salisbury was stunned. For years she had been travelling the world, but hadn't really seen it. She had been isolated in a glass bubble of protection that kept her carefully walled off from poverty. She finally began asking herself the questions that had been slowly bubbling up, "Who am

I? Where am I? What am I doing with my life? What does all this mean? Why am I here?"

For Salisbury, it was a defining moment.

"I think this realization of a disconnect was my epiphany."

Up to this point, her life had been lived according to a checklist defined by society. It hadn't brought satisfaction. It was time for a drastic change and the one that presented itself was totally unexpected.

Over the next ten months, her recent marriage fell apart. Her husband thought it was a midlife crisis and that a little time away would get it out of her system. Salisbury didn't know how to explain what was happening inside. The change had come overnight and the woman she had been when he married her no longer existed.

At the same time, an old friend and partner in crime came back into her life—Graeme Belshaw. "He was a guy I met through business. Most Saturdays we would go out and have fun. We were both into extreme things, so we would ring each other up and say, 'Hey, have you ever been in a hot air balloon? Let's go do it. Hey, have you ever been gliding? Let's go.' His wife and my husband weren't interested in doing stuff like that, so we'd go out and do it—crazy things, like the scariest rides at the fair."

Belshaw had just left his wife and Salisbury's marriage was on the rocks, so they were in a similar space. When she asked what he was going to do next, his answer was, "Make a load of money, buy a boat, and sail around the world."

Perfect! She already had money to buy the boat and was ready to throw caution to the wind. Societal expectations were tossed out the window. This open door offered a chance to escape the predictable future that lay ahead, and with a friend she enjoyed. She still remembers the moment when reality hit. "We were laughing and joking about it. Then I'm driving home and I start thinking, 'This is actually quite a good idea.' That was pretty much it. It only took a couple of weeks to decide."

The first stop was South Africa. Belshaw had travelled extensively and had even been a delivery skipper. He felt Africa was a brilliant starting point because the exchange rate was very favourable at the time, making the cost of a boat about a third of the price it would be in England, and the work needed to make it seaworthy would be much more affordable. It was also a better starting point for their journey to begin.

They landed in Pretoria in September 1998, then headed down to Durban where they purchased a Colin Archer 45-foot Double-ender—a sturdy ocean-going steel cruiser. It took six months to prep the boat to sail around the world. They had to seal any leaks, purchase a freezer for food storage, and add equipment such as navigational aids. The day soon came when the work was done and they sailed out of Richard's Bay into their new life.

Salisbury was surprised by how different life was. "I didn't realize until we left the harbour how protected we had been. You're safe when you're in the marina, but South Africa is a very violent place."

After leaving Africa, the couple headed over to Madagascar and spent three months exploring. It was another eye-opener. "There are no tourists or roads on the west coast where we were, so the only people who get to see these towns are sailors or people who arrive by boat. The environment was like a hundred years ago. I learned a lot there in terms of a very different way of living. It was beautiful."

All along the way, Salisbury was acquiring the skills necessary to survive away from civilization. Living on a boat means self-sufficiency and that comes from knowledge: how much food, what kind of food, how much water, navigational skills, medical information, how to make jam and safely bottle meat, and what items are best for trade with other sailors. This was pre-internet and pre-GPS, so the couple turned to books and old-school navigation methods.

"Our boat's library held books on everything we might need to know—it was our knowledge base. We learned how to navigate by using a compass and parallel lines on maps—no sextant."

Having a basic knowledge of medicine and time-tested aromatherapy remedies was particularly important as there would be many times they were far away from outside help. This came in handy when Salisbury contracted malaria in East Africa. She knew her body, recognized the symptoms immediately, and wasted no time starting treatment before getting the important blood test needed to verify her suspicion.

"I had the remedy on the boat already in case I experienced the symptoms at sea and took the first tablet before

I even went for the blood test. A half day wasted on the blood test is another day the malaria can multiple. The main reason I got the test was to get official confirmation so my friends could take action. People in close proximity have a high chance of getting malaria at the same time—the mosquito bites you and then infects next person he bites."

She has never had a recurrence.

The biggest challenge of Salisbury's and Belshaw's journey in self-sufficiency was the Indian Ocean. It would take six months to cross. The sailing times were brutal. There were long stretches of sailing twenty-four hours a day when someone had to be at the helm every moment and there was only the two of them to share the responsibility. A shift change had to be made every two hours and by the end, the sleep deprivation took its toll. In the middle of crossing this ocean was a three-month stay on an isolated island with other sailors, followed by another twenty-four hour a day, seventeen-day passage to reach Thailand.

Preparation was important. You could only take so much—water, fuel, fresh and prepared food—and that dominated a full six months of preparation time. There was no desalinization plant to provide water, so how would they collect rain water and store it? How much flour, sugar, garlic, etcetera, should they buy? How much fresh food should they preserve? Would the other sailors they meet on the island in the middle of the Indian Ocean have goods to trade that would fill out what they might be lacking?

In the end, this stopover on the British Indian Ocean Territory Islands was a lesson in community that struck a chord for Salisbury.

"There was no way you could survive there by yourself. There was no fresh water and the islands were literally just sand and coconuts. We would get on the radio every morning and have a market. 'I've got garlic left, but need onions. I've got pickles, but does anyone have spare fish hooks.'"

Salisbury became known for her rice wine and ginger beer, always a welcome distraction. To keep it in stock meant they had to carry lots of sugar—twenty kilos at that point.

One would think claustrophobia would set in living on a boat, but what she remembers is just the opposite. "Your back garden is the world. If you think of outside the boat, your world is massive. There are no fences. It doesn't matter that you can't step off the deck for a walk. The world, the sky, and the ocean are so big that you don't feel small. You're just inside the boat to sleep. It's yours and you can see right to the horizon."

When the couple arrived in Thailand, they only had forty dollars to their names. The solution was to offer charter outings to backpackers. Belshaw had always functioned as skipper and Salisbury as first mate in their travels. Anything to do with business—bookings, food, money collection, and outings of interest—were under the first mate's umbrella. As a result, the new responsibilities fell firmly on her shoulders. Getting clients to step outside their comfort zone and try new things was a big part of making the new venture a success.

"When we started doing the charters, I looked after the

guests and did all the trips and sales. We would take six to eight people for up to ten days. I would teach them all about this lifestyle and about community. I encouraged people to do things they had never done before. We had a lot of non-swimmers and I would get them to put life jackets on and go snorkeling. We'd go hiking. There were a lot of first-time experiences."

Salisbury thought she had finally found her purpose. "As far as I was concerned, this was my life. I had my community and I could teach people. I only realized recently, this was my training for my new publishing community."

The couple had become friends with benefits who lived a nomadic life travelling the world. They explored the beauty and wonder of nature almost daily. A sense of community and purpose filled her days. She was content, but fate had other things in store. One day, Belshaw announced it was time she left the boat. He wanted more from a relationship. He wanted romance and all that that entailed. Salisbury was devastated at being set adrift. Backpacking by herself in the Asian triangle—Thailand, Laos, and Cambodia—offered a welcome distraction.

"I was travelling by myself, but would hook up with other single travellers. I had no friends, no home, no job—I didn't know where I belonged in the world. I didn't want to go back to England. It wasn't home and I didn't fit into that lifestyle. The boat was my home. I was so lost."

Creating a budget from what money she had left only allowed expenditures of ten dollars a day, just enough at that time for a backpacker to live on. Salisbury figured she could travel about six months before running out of money. All along the way, the physical demands of carrying a heavy pack took their toll as her scoliosis meant constant pain, but there were always generous locals.

One day a Good Samaritan stepped in to help her make an important travel connection. After arriving in Thailand, she was trying to get to Bangkok and was in a desperate hurry to get to the train on time as it only ran once every three days. Salisbury threw caution to the wind.

"I arrived by boat and a little motorbike taxi driver came straight up to me, grabbed my bag, which was huge, and said, 'Where are you going?' I had no idea, only that I had to catch this particular bus, but I decided to trust him. He put me on his little moped and set off. He's looking over the top of my bag while driving, and I was riding side-saddle, because you had to ride this way in Thailand if you're a lady. Twenty minutes later we arrived at the station only to find the regular passenger bus was full. A Thai woman already on the bus ended up getting off the bus so I could have her seat. It is still a strong memory of karma and to this day I give backpackers my bus tickets if they are begging."

The journey continued when she arrived at the train station as there were only first class tickets left—a price way outside her budget. "I had to make an instant decision. I ran to an ATM machine to get enough money to pay for the first class ticket, and by that time they had already put my bag on the train and it was ready to leave. The conductor sat me in first class and then invited me to sit with him."

This courtesy and willingness to help a stranger was true of most people she met in Southeast Asia.

The nomadic lifestyle was wearing thin. Six months of travelling in a crowd usually much younger had brought weariness. Depression set in. Salisbury checked into a cheap hotel that seemed like luxury after sleeping in garlic fields. Then she had an episode with her back that left her in tremendous pain. It was not a proud moment.

"I can't even tell you how bad it was. For two weeks, I lay in my room crying, trying to figure out what I was going to do with my life. I couldn't even feed myself or get a bottle of water. My goal every day was to crawl out of my room and get to the internet cafe and send out help messages. I was alone and no one would come—not even Belshaw. In the end, a Canadian I had met backpacking came to my rescue. She nursed me back to health over a three-week period."

It was in Canada where Salisbury would finally find her purpose and it all began on a dock in Nanaimo, British Columbia. A Canadian woman met through a sailing website—a writer—offered the world traveller a place to stay on her sailboat. Salisbury accepted.

Those first memories of arriving in Canada are still very clear. "I arrived in February and was overwhelmed by the beauty. I was on the ferry and looking at the blue sky. Even though it was cold, I enjoyed the feeling of the sun warming my body instead of baking my skin. I had really missed this—the seasons and the beauty. It was all so alive and green. I didn't realize how much I'd missed."

As she was walked up the dock to the woman's boat, a man was watching her through the portal of his own boat.

His name was Greg and he would change her life.

Salisbury still says that if you're a single, attractive woman with no money and no home, walk into a marina. It's full of very single men. Greg showed up within minutes holding a bottle of wine. Within three days, they were living together and enjoying the wonders of a new relationship. Inside, a door long shut finally opened. This was the passion she had long desired—a deeper connection that illuminated what she had been missing. This was a man unlike any others.

"Greg is the first man I ever met who actually stops and smells the roses. Even though I'd been travelling the world for four years, I'd been doing it by myself. This was the very first time I was actually sharing an experience with someone. Greg pulled out of me what my passion was, who I was, and what I wanted out of life."

The next two years were again nomadic. Being in Canada on a visitor's visa meant there was a six-month limit to her stay. Off they sailed to Mexico. When they ran out of money, the couple flew to England. Greg didn't have a working visa so spent his time as a tourist. Salisbury quickly landed a job with Peter Sage, who built and then sold companies.

"He was a serial entrepreneur who was launching a brand new business and said, 'We're going to take this from zero to a million in three months. When we do, you will get X amount of commission and I will fly all the management staff to the only seven star hotel in the world—in Dubai—for the weekend.'"

Salisbury worked hard to help build the company, but in the end she passed on the trip. Greg's visa was expiring and she chose instead to accompany him back to Mexico.

The couple was ready to let go of their nomadic life. They chose to settle in Canada and for Julie to be allowed to stay, that meant a wedding. Well, maybe two weddings. Greg had already proposed a year and a half earlier in England, rose in hand. Now was the perfect time. Seventeen of Greg's relatives were invited to a Christmas Eve celebration. Salisbury's last boss, Peter Sage, had since immigrated to Canada and offered them the use of his beautiful mansion in the British Properties of West Vancouver. It had a big spiral staircase, a huge fireplace, an enormous dining table, and a hot tub. The view overlooked the whole city, which, at that time of year, was encased in rain and fog. The home, however, was situated completely above the clouds.

The second wedding was a summer ceremony on Dallas Road Beach in Victoria with Salisbury's family. This was a childhood vision come to life. "My dream was a horse and carriage, a gypsy outfit, flowers in my hair, a marriage on the beach, and then a picnic in the park. My whole family was there, about twenty of us altogether. Everyone was picked up in three horse and carriages. Then all the guests went down to the beach and built an arbour out of driftwood decorated with wild sweet peas. They moved the logs around to sit on. It was beautiful. We did a sand ceremony and still have the sand today."

This relationship would provide exactly the supportive foundation the future publisher needed to move into what would become her life purpose.

Early on, Salisbury had been encouraged to keep a journal of her travels. The twelve months it took to complete her immigration process in Canada offered the perfect time to develop this journal into a book. *A Seven Year Journey Around the World: Discovering My Passion and Purpose* launched in April 2008. At the same time, she began to develop a manual to help other writer share their own stories. It became the foundation for her InspireABook workshops.

Teaching others how to bring their books to publication meant having completed books that needed a publisher. Salisbury next stepped into the role of literary agent. A UK publisher was signed to handle all her titles and the company's owner started to train both she and Greg on how to run his imprint publishing business in Canada. Then one day, he emailed to say he was too busy to continue, but he offered to help the couple with the transition to creating their own independent label and would hand over all his connections to ease their way. It was a very stressful moment.

"When he told me he couldn't publish my books, I had a meltdown. I had three launch dates planned. But Greg was already helping our authors with their websites and it ended up being an easy transition for him to be trained in the needed skill set. He just dived in and became my hero. That's when everything took off. We have now published over fifty titles."

The couple had become more than husband and wife. They were a team in business, working toward a common goal.

As the business grew, Salisbury's back pain became an

ever increasing issue. For years she had been able to just ignore it and live life any way she chose. That now came to an end.

"In 2010, it was time to take my workshops to the next level. There were a couple of workshops when I was in so much pain by the end, I wasn't sure I could run a business. It was time to see a specialist and see what my options were."

The decision was a hard one as up to that moment, all drugs had been off the table. That personal choice now had to be reconsidered. In the end, the best solution embraced exercise, stress reduction, lifestyle changes, and some medication.

December 2013 was another crucial time. Business had grown more quickly than income and the demands on Salisbury stretched her to her limits both personally and financially. There were a few high profile authors in the process of signing with Influence Publishing who would require even more commitment. It was time to take a step back and regroup. A vacation was in order.

"I decided to take three weeks off in December 2013 to recharge, spend some much needed time with my husband, and reconnect with my best friend from Cambodia. We arranged to rent an apartment in Mexico. It was a time of reflection, relaxation, and leaving the office to run without me for three weeks. I had only limited contact with the office every day, so it really showed me the strengths and weaknesses of my staff."

Another important trip came three months later, to

Dubai, to attend a week-long business workshop run by her former boss, serial entrepreneur Peter Sage. Attendees were encouraged to experience the millionaire lifestyle, dream big, and do things outside their comfort zone. Salisbury found it life-changing.

"Not only did I achieve my lifelong dream of jumping out of an airplane, I developed a whole new mindset of what I was capable of achieving. I didn't need to give away my business control to any partners. I am capable of doing it all. I have the leadership skills and creative imagination to take my business to the next level. By the end of the week, I had very clear goals and I set a new intention to move forward with the business the way I knew was best."

Within a week of returning to Canada, she began to implement changes. Influence Publishing's cutting-edge business model needed a distributor that was open to a new way of looking at things.

"I had a deep knowing that the right distributor was out there; we simply had not connected yet. When you are in the flow, when your intentions are that clear, when you come from a place of "knowing"—it just requires patience. These things cannot be rushed."

A perfect match was found when she met Eric Kampmann of Midpoint books out of New York. Once an agreement was signed, things began to move very quickly. Influence Publishing now has a partner that can take their strong titles into the lucrative US market—all the big chain stores, grocery stores, libraries, and airport retail outlets.

Looking back over her journey, Salisbury embraces all

the steps that led to this moment in time—product development, handling charters on the boat, dealing with limitations, and personal hardship. Success is measured in terms of mentoring wisdom leaders to share their stories; this is her life's purpose. These writers also offer a welcome community to be a part of—something she also offers them in return—and at home is a life partner to share and support this journey.

Whatever challenges life brings next, Salisbury is ready to meet them head on.

"There are no longer any obstacles, just turns in the river that I am navigating as they appear. There is always a way around, over, or through. The river always flows. I'm now going with that flow, not fighting against it! The world is my oyster and I see Influence Publishing becoming a real force to be reckoned with! Nothing will get in my way!"

Author Biography

Marilyn R. Wilson is a freelance writer and editor with a passion for interviewing. Whether through a random encounter on the New York subway or via a "one-on-one" with an internationally recognized artist, the goal is the same—to share the unique journeys of inspiring individuals. In 2007, this goal led the author to co-launch a successful, innovative magazine focused on professionals working in the fashion industry, paired with photography and illustrations by local artists. Now on staff at *Raine Magazine* (NY/Miami/LA) as well as freelancing for other publications, Wilson has taken her passion to a new audience with the release of her first book.

Writer ~ Author ~ Editor

Current Positions:
International Assistant Editor, Raine Magazine
www.rainemagazine.com
Contributing Writer, Metro-Living-Zine
www.metrolivingzine.com
Member B.C. Travel Writer's Association
www.bcatw.org/marilyn-r-wilson/

Website:
www.oliobymarilyn.com

Social Media:
Facebook
www.facebook.com/MarilynRWilsonWriter
Twitter
www.twitter.com/oliobymarilyn
LinkedIn
ca.linkedin.com/pub/marilyn-r-wilson/10/b62/117/
WattPad
www.wattpad.com/MarilynRWilson

If you want to get on the path to be a published author
with Influence Publishing please go to
www.InfluencePublishing.com

Inspiring books that influence change

More information on our other titles and how to submit
your own proposal can be found at
www.InfluencePublishing.com

CPSIA information can be obtained at www.ICGtesting.com
Printed in the USA
LVOW10s0429091214

417841LV00013B/52/P